MOUNTING
METHODS

BY VIVIAN C. KISTLER, CPF, GCF

COLUMBA PUBLISHING CO.
154 Pembroke Rd.
Akron, Ohio 44333

Library of Professional Picture Framing
Volume Five
Mounting Methods
by Vivian Carli Kistler, CPF, GCF

Published by Columba Publishing Co. Inc.
Akron, Ohio USA
Copyright 2005, 2002, 1999
All rights reserved
Revised Edition 2005
First Edition 1999
Manufactured in the United States of America
ISBN 0-938655-04-3

10 9 8 7 6 5 4 3

Editors:
    Vivian Carli Kistler
    Sheri Leigh Galat
    Carli Kistler Miller

PrePress:
    Carli Kistler Miller

Illustrations:
    Kelly Ross

Photograph Credits:
    Nannette Bedway
    Carli Kistler-Miller
    Allan Lamb
    Heather Protz
    Barbara Schlueter

Framers whose work
appears in this book:
    Carolyn Birchenall, CPF
    Jim Cook, CPF
    Allan Lamb, CPF
    Brian Wolf, CPF, GCF

Illustrations on pages 12 and 21 were reprinted with per-
mission from *How to Build Frameshop Worktables, Fixtures
& Jigs* by Paul MacFarland. Columba Publishing Co.
ISBN 0-938655-36-1

Special Thanks
to the following framers, who have graciously con-
tributed their expertise to this book:
    • Donna & Steve Albin for their help with wet
      mounting.
    • Allan Lamb, CPF for his advice on mounting
      photography.
    • Robert Mayfield, CPF, GCF for his help with
      pricing.
    • William Parker, CPF, GCF for his advice on
      volume mounting.
    • Paul MacFarland, CPF, GCF for his drawing
      of worktables and his explanation of static
      mounting.

MOUNTING
METHODS

VOLUME 5
OF THE
LIBRARY OF PROFESSIONAL PICTURE FRAMING

COLUMBA PUBLISHING COMPANY
AKRON, OHIO 44313

TradeMarks & Registrations

This book contains many registered and trademarked products. Every effort has been made to identify the holder of this registration and to properly identify the product manufacturer.

Trademarks and brand names used throughout this book are identified with the appropriate symbol at first mention; thereafter the name may or may not carry the registration or trademark symbol in the text or drawings.

Library of Professional Picture Framing
Vol 1 Picture Framing
Vol 2 Mat Cutting & Decoration
Vol 3 Framing Needlework
Vol 4 Conservation Framing
Vol 5 Mounting Methods
Vol 6 Framing Photography

Acknowledgements

We would like to thank to the following framers and companies for providing information and encouraging development of education in the picture framing industry.

John Alley
Bienfang Mounting Products
Patricia Bradley, CPF
William Bradley, CPF
Crescent Cardboard Co.
Diane Day, CPF
Decor Magazine
Drytac Corporation
Elmer's Framing Products, Inc.
Jocelyn Flament, CPF
Paul Frederick, CPF
Filmolux, USA
Lineco, Inc.
Connie Henshaw
Hot Press
Steve Kocsis, CPF
Larson-Juhl
James Lofink
Nielsen Bainbridge
Chris Paschke, CPF, GCF
Picture Framing Magazine
Print Mount Co.
Professional Picture Framers Assoc.
Savage Universal Corp.
Slater Todd, CPF
Billy Sproles
3M Office Supply Division
Tru Vue, Inc.
Jeff Wanee, CPF

CONTENTS

CHAPTER 1

MOUNTING BASICS

MOUNTING

Gravity, moisture, and pressure can cause cockling, buckling, wrinkling, and warping of framed paper art. The purpose of mounting is to control these effects, by suspending the article in the frame with hinges, supports or with full mounting.

Although hinges and edge supports are discussed briefly on pages 14-15, the focus of this book is full mounting techniques, in which the entire surface of the artwork is bonded to a substrate.

Full mounting is not a conservation technique. The rigid standards of conservation framing require reversibility of all procedures and techniques with no alteration of the artwork. Despite claims of reversibility and removability on some mounting products, many require potentially harmful solvents, and leave behind residue of adhesive and solvents after removal. The action of removal may cause damage. New products are developed for picture framing every year, and reversible mounting adhesives that come onto the market should be investigated. However, traditional framers are reluctant to embrace new products until the products have proven themselves over time.

Even though full mounting is generally considered non-reversible, this does not mean that the quality of mounting materials and techniques is unimportant. It is still necessary to consider the integrity of the artwork, and to choose mounting methods that will not be harmful to it. With the archival quality mounting adhesives and boards available, picture framers can easily produce mounting that meets most measures of conservation *except* reversibility.

For a frame shop that offers mounting services, it is important to keep a variety of substrates and adhesives on hand because in mounting, as in other framing methods, there is not one method that will fit all projects.

In addition to full mounting of paper art, other mounting processes can be useful in the frame shop, such as canvas transfer, which can transform a reproduction of a painting into a textured image that simulates a painting on canvas.

Lamination is an important variation of the mounting process, providing surface protection for a variety of art such as maps, photos and reproductions.

TYPES OF MOUNTING METHODS

FULL MOUNTING METHODS

DRY MOUNTING
The application of artwork or fabric to a substrate using heat-activated adhesives in a heat press.

PRESSURE-SENSITIVE MOUNTING
Bonding artwork or fabric to a substrate using an adhesive that activates under pressure. Can be used with or without a press.

WET MOUNTING
Bonding artwork or fabric to a substrate using wet glues and pastes with a press or weight.

SPRAY MOUNTING
The application of artwork or fabric to a substrate using glues applied with aerosol sprays. Can be used with or without a press.

LAMINATING
Heat or pressure-sensitive application of a protective clear vinyl or polyester film to the surface of a reproduction, photograph, or other paper.

CANVAS TRANSFER
Transferring a printed image from paper to canvas to simulate a painting on canvas. This can be done using most reproductions and photographs.

SUSPENSION METHODS

General practice and conservation methods may include the use of corners, pockets, hinges and tapes to secure work to a back board. Detailed directions and explanations are fully explained in *Vol.4, Conservation Framing.*

STRETCHING

This method is used with needlework and fabrics, and includes lacing, pinning, and stapling to substrates. These methods are fully explored in *Vol.3, Needlework Framing.*

THE BASIC PRINCIPLES OF MOUNTING

There are a few basic concepts that apply to all types of mounting. The traditional foursome are Time, Temperature, Pressure, and Moisture. These variable elements are to be considered regardless of the mounting method chosen.

TIME

Time is a key factor in successful mounting. Heat-activated adhesives require sufficient time for the heat to travel through the materials, activate the adhesive and create a bond. In a vacuum press time is required to pull moisture from the materials and create the pressure necessary for the bond. Wet pastes require evaporation time. Pressure-sensitive adhesives have an initial grip but bond permanently over a period of 3 to 24 hours.

TEMPERATURE

The appropriate temperature for dry mounting is hot enough to activate the adhesive but not so hot that it would damage the item being mounted. Time and temperature work together in the mounting process—the hotter the adhesive the less time is required to bond; the cooler the adhesive the longer the period of time for the bond.

Extreme temperatures can also affect cold mount materials, wet pastes and spray adhesives as well as storage of all mounting adhesives. Excessive cold can cause drying, brittleness and other unwanted effects, while an excessively hot environment can cause softening or even melting of adhesives.

PRESSURE

Pressure is part of all mounting processes, from the gentle rubbing of a finger to adhere a piece of tape, to the intense pressure of a vacuum press. Controlled, even pressure is the key to a complete bond.

MOISTURE

The first three elements (Time, Temperature, and Pressure) combine in various ratios to form the basis of all mounting methods. The successful interplay of these elements can be disrupted or even ruined by the influence of the often ignored fourth element, moisture.

Humidity is absorbed into all porous paper products, including artwork, substrates, and some mounting adhesives. Moisture trapped in the mounting package may cause blisters and bubbles. Moisture can prevent cold mount adhesives from bonding. Predrying of materials (in a heat press) will reduce most moisture problems in mounting.

TIME
•
TEMPERATURE
•
PRESSURE
•
MOISTURE

POROSITY

The porosity or breathability of materials is an important factor in mounting. Porous materials allow air and moisture to pass through. The porosity of the item that will be mounted, the bonding agent that will be used, and the substrate beneath them should all be considered when making mounting decisions.

It is important that some elements in the mounting package are porous, so that trapped air and moisture can find a pathway out of the package. In fact, the more porosity the better. For example, if the artwork to be mounted is a non-porous paper like an RC photograph, it would be best to use both a porous substrate and a porous adhesive.

Mounting adhesives and films are usually clearly identified as porous or non-porous. Most papers and boards are porous. To identify non-porous substrates look for clues like slick and/or high gloss surfaces, hard, dense materials like masonite or glass, or plasticized finishes. Use the same criteria for judging the porosity of artwork. When in doubt about the porosity of the art, use a porous substrate.

WHAT TO MOUNT • WHAT NOT TO MOUNT
MOUNTING CHOICES • MAKING DECISIONS

It is physically possible to mount any paper item. The challenge is deciding whether a particular item should be fully mounted, and if so, which method would be best.

The artwork itself will provide many of the clues needed to make mounting decisions. Since full mounting is not considered a conservation technique, any piece that requires conservation framing will not be mounted. This includes original artwork (including limited edition works), original certificates, and any item that may need to be completely "unframed" any time in the future.

Of course there are exceptions. One of those exceptions concerns fine art photography. Many photographers insist on having their photos mounted as a matter of course. Let them assist in the mounting decisions, because they know about the printing method and paper that were used to produce the photo. Use fine-quality adhesives and substrates.

Artists working in other media, such as pencil or watercolor, may also want to have their work mounted. The artist who created the work does have the right to make decisions about its handling. Picture framers can help artists by explaining methods and materials that will be friendliest to their artwork.

Surface texture is another characteristic that can make mounting impractical. All full mounting methods involve some degree of pressure on the artwork. If pressure might flatten embossed areas or break surface features of the art, it should not be mounted.

Once it is determined that a work will be mounted, the method and materials must be chosen. Again, look to the artwork for guidance. What is the medium? Will it be affected by heat? How much heat? There are mounting tissues and films that operate at relatively low temperatures, and others that need additional heat.

Consider the possible affects of moisture. Will wet pastes affect the medium? Think about the surface quality of printed work. Is there a glossy finish that may be affected by mounting techniques?

When choosing a substrate and adhesive, look at the back of the artwork. Is it bumpy, or rough, or slick and shiny? How heavy and thick is the artwork? Is the substrate stable enough to restrict it from reacting to gravity and humidity? The answers will affect which materials are most suitable.

Although it may seem as though there is a lot to consider, the relative permanence of full mounting makes it worthwhile to think about these factors before proceeding. Most of your mounting projects will be ordinary and trouble-free, but knowing how to handle the difficult pieces is the key to mounting with confidence.

> ### DO NOT MOUNT:
> *Original art, pen or pencil drawings, charcoals, pastels, watercolors, investment pieces, limited edition art, historical documents, antiques, and sentimental artifacts. Do not heat mount "thermo" or other heat-sensitive items. Do not mount anything that may need to be in "mint condition" at a later date.*

HANDLING THE "SHOULD NOTS"

If an artist or other owner of artwork insists that an item be mounted against the framer's advise, two options exist: refuse the job, or agree to do the mounting and ask the customer to sign a disclaimer or release form.

REFUSE THE JOB
Refusing the customer really goes against the grain of custom framing. After all, the whole concept of "custom" is based on the notion of work done to the buyer's specifications. However, every custom profession has its standards, and must adhere to them to maintain a good reputation. Make sure the customer understands why the mounting will not be performed, and explain why the alternatives suggested are important for the integrity and/or safety of the art.

DISCLAIMERS
No need for a long, harsh legal document. Use simple, clear, non-threatening language. A statement such as, "Although the risks and consequences of this procedure have been explained to me, I have elected to have it done," and include a line for identifying the art and mounting procedure in question, plus a line for the customer to sign and date the form.

CHOOSING SUBSTRATES
COLOR, TEXTURE, QUALITY

The substrate is the underlying support to which artwork is mounted. A number of factors affect the best choice of substrate for a particular project.

Each characteristic of the substrate—the look, the feel, and the internal composition—can affect the artwork that will be mounted to it.

Thin or translucent papers can be brightened or darkened depending on the color of the board beneath them.

Texture may create a pleasing effect, or a very smooth surface may be important.

The mounted piece may be intended for temporary display, or may be a sentimental poster that needs to last a long time.

The thickness, rigidity, and density of the substrate is also important. Large, thin boards will keep artwork flat while in horizontal shelves, but the entire board may warp when put into the frame. A thick, soft board might seem rigid, but may buckle in high humidity. Foam center boards dent easily.

Consider all of these aspects when choosing the substrate for a mounting project.

Each characteristic of the substrate— the look, the feel, and the internal composition—can affect the artwork that will be mounted to it.

SUBSTRATES
REGULAR MATBOARD
Regular matboard has a buffered acid-free pulp core and backing paper. It is available in an extensive color range with many different surface textures and finishes. The texture and color may interfere with the mounting process. Matboards may not be thick or rigid enough for some mounting purposes.

WHITE CORE MATBOARD
This board has acid-free surface papers and a white core and lining paper. Better quality than regular matboards but not as good as museum or conservation boards. Can be used for mounting projects but be careful of the influence of texture and color from surface papers.

MUSEUM MATBOARD
Often referred to as rag mat, a museum board is made of 100% pure cotton fiber. It is naturally acid- and lignin-free. It is available buffered or unbuffered. Unbuffered rag board is used for the mounting and matting of certain photographs such as chromogenic, albumen, dye transfer, cyanotypes and other alkaline sensitive articles. Cotton rag matboard is the traditional favorite of museum conservators.

CONSERVATION MATBOARD
A buffered mat and mount board made from purified wood pulp, with buffered acid-free surface and lining papers. Acceptable for most conservation purposes. Offered in a wide variety of colored surface papers. Remember to consider the effects of color and texture when using these boards for mounting.

EXTRA SMOOTH MOUNTING BOARD
A bright white, ultra-smooth surface on a rigid core. Constructed from multiple layers of very dense, compressed white refined wood fibers. Surface and core are non-yellowing and acid-free. Excellent for mounting high-gloss photos and glossy artwork, or whenever ultra-smoothness is important.

WHITE SURFACE MOUNTING BOARD
This board has a solid news core with a double-sided, smooth, buffered, acid-free, white surface. Used for routine mounting. A good substrate for general mounting applications.

ACID-FREE WHITE MOUNTING BOARD
This is a double-sided, white core, buffered, acid-free mounting board. This board may be used with all mounting methods.

RECYCLED MOUNTING BOARDS
Made using 100% recycled fibers. They are white on both sides with the recycled symbol imprint on one side. Available in single and double thickness. All components of are buffered with calcium carbonate to be pH neutral.

ALL BLACK MOUNTING BOARD
Solid black throughout and both sides are usable. Black mounting board is excellent for mounting photographs and newspaper.

COMPETITION MOUNTING BOARD
A triple-thick (.120) board designed especially for photography competitions. Meets Professional Photographers of America exhibition mounting requirement for thickness and size. Solid black or double-sided white.

NEWS MOUNTING BOARD
This very dense, rigid, solid core board is grayish in color and is composed of recycled materials. Because of its color and acidity of its components, it should not be used as a mounting board by professional framers. Chipboard is similar in content and characteristics.

CORRUGATED BOARD
The fluted core makes this type of board unsuitable for mounting projects. Do Not Use for mounting purposes.

FOAM BOARDS
Foam center board is a lightweight, inert, white, plastic center faced on both sides with white clay-coated paper. Available in several thicknesses, framers typically use 1/8", 3/16", 1/4" and 1/2". Available in standard 32x40", 40x60" and 4'x8' sheets. Some companies offer foam board with color centers and surfaces. Black is especially useful for mounting projects.

It is very important to use foam board intended for the picture framing industry. The type used in the construction industry has different standards of composition that may cause trouble. For example, construction foam board often has an inconsistent density in its plastic core, which may collapse in spots during mounting. Also avoid foam boards with cores composed of styrofoam "beads", similar to the composition of styrofoam cups.

Although foam board makes a good substrate for mounting, it can be adversely affected by excessive heat. Depending on the brand, foam board may begin to soften and bend somewhere between 185°F and 200°F. If the mounting adhesive requires temperatures in this range or higher, test the foam board before using it for mounting.

ACID-FREE FOAM BOARD
Acid-free foam center board is faced on both sides with off-white, acid-free barrier papers. It is available in several thicknesses and sizes, and can be used with all mounting methods.

RAG FOAM BOARD
This board has 100% cotton rag papers on both sides of its inert plastic center.

HEAVY DUTY FOAM BOARD
This board has a dense polystyrene core that resists moisture, denting, crushing, warping, and bending. The smooth paper surface accepts glues and adhesives. An underlaminate layer of polyethylene beneath the paper surface acts as a moisture barrier that prevents bowing and twisting. Rigid and durable. Good when strength and/or humidity resistance are important. White or black. 32x40" to 48x96". Some heavy duty foam boards are available precoated with heat-activated or pressure-sensitive adhesive.

HEAVY DUTY FOAM BOARD WITH WOOD FIBER VENEER
Rigid polystyrene foam with wood fiber veneer laminate applied to both sides resulting in a strong, durable board. Smooth and warp-resistant, it is a sturdy support for oversized mountings, but the acidity of the wood veneer limits its use in professional framing. Special board cutters are required. Available in white, natural and black in several thicknesses and sizes.

SUBSTRATES COATED WITH ADHESIVES
Some mounting substrates are available precoated with adhesives. The substrates are foam boards or rigid mounting boards; the adhesives are heat-activated or pressure-sensitive. These products offer convenience, and several of them offer additional features, such as low-temperature heat mounting, or reversibility

OTHER SUBSTRATE MATERIALS
In addition to the boards typically used in picture framing, other materials can be used for mounting. Test the chosen adhesive to make sure a secure bond will be achieved before performing the mounting.

MASONITE®
Porous, smooth or textured boards composed of compressed wood fibers and binding materials. Brown in color. Rigid, 1/8" and 1/4" thickness. Not suitable for most mounting projects because of its composition.

GLASS
Used for decorative mounting applications, especially with laminates for faux glass etching and mirror designing. Pictures may be mounted to glass for a decorator look.

ACRYLIC SHEETS
An acrylic sheet such as Plexiglas®, can be used for mounting with pressure-sensitive adhesives and some porous dry mount tissues.

FABRIC
Linen canvas, cotton duck, or thin cotton sheeting can be mounted to the back of artwork as reinforcement or used to create the look of a painting. Some fabrics come precoated with adhesive, such as ArtShield Mapbak™ from Drytac.

STORAGE OF BOARDS

The ideal mounting board is flat, clean, and dry. Boards are susceptible to the effects of gravity and moisture. They can become coated with dust and dirt. They can become dented or even bent.

Proper storage will help minimize these effects. Frame shops are often too busy with day-to-day operations to pay attention to dust and slumping boards, but a great deal of attention will be paid to fixing these preventable problems.

Boards can be stored horizontally or vertically. For mounting boards and matboards, most storage units need to accommodate 32x40" boards, with an additional space provided for oversized boards and their scraps. Storage units should allow a minimum of 2" of clearance for each dimension, so a unit for 32x40" boards needs to be at least 34x42". Convenient slots can be built beneath your framing tables, or separate units can be bought or built.

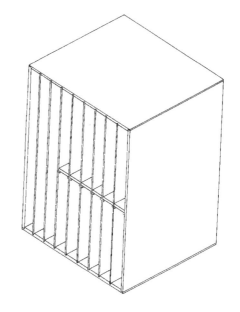

Keep like-sized boards together, with the scraps gathered in their own section, to minimize wear and tear on the full-sized boards.

Control excess humidity in the shop with dehumidifiers and air conditioners. Humidity can be damaging to all papers and fibers, so controlled humidity is important for all of the boards, papers, and fabrics in your shop, including customer artwork.

Do not store boards directly on a concrete floor because the concrete holds moisture which will be absorbed by the boards. The boards can be raised by setting a pallet on the floor, covered with a sheet of foam center board.

Keeping boards in storage units will help keep them clean, but it is impossible to keep boards completely dust free. Use a sponge slightly dampened with clear water to clean a dusty board. A dampened sponge may also clean scuff marks and raise smashed fibers in dented areas on a board.

RELEASE MATERIALS

by Robert Mayfield, CPF, GCF

Release materials, as they are used in picture framing, are sheets to which adhesives will not stick. These specially treated materials are used to protect the mounting equipment and the artwork being mounted by preventing the transfer of adhesives and other contamination.

As harmless as release papers appear, they can create static electricity which attracts dust and dirt. Some printing inks and art mediums transfer to the release paper when subjected to heat. These could then be deposited on the next item being mounted. Get in the habit of checking the release paper after each use.

The basic types of release materials used in the framing industry are paper, plastic and boards which are covered with a release agent such as silicone or Teflon®. Release materials should be replaced when they become damaged or worn. Release materials will only produce smooth, clean results if they are clean and wrinkle-free.

RELEASE PAPERS

Release papers are available either single- or double-sided in several sizes and weights. Single-sided release paper often has a light blue tint on the coated side to help distinguish it from the uncoated side. Double-sided release paper should not be used with oversized formats since it is slippery and limp and prone to folding.

Wrinkles or creases in the release paper will transfer to the artwork that is being mounted. Inspect the release paper before every use for wrinkles, dirt and adhesive tissue. If any of these flaws are found, the release coating is starting to fail and should be replaced with a new piece of release paper.

RELEASE BOARDS

A release board is made by applying a single-sided release paper to a rigid substrate. Release boards may be purchased, or may be made in the frame shop.

Release boards are less prone to wrinkling and may last longer than release papers, but additional dwell time is required to allow the heat to transfer through the board and activate the adhesive. Release boards can help prevent "platen lines" on oversized pieces mounted in a mechanical press.

TIPS FOR USING RELEASE MATERIALS

- Release papers are often kept in use well beyond their lifetime. Replace release materials as soon as they are contaminated or wrinkled.

- Mount projects using a release envelope similar in size to the desired size of the finished product.

- Clearly mark the rolls of release papers. Some brands look very much like adhesive tissues and may be mistaken for one another.

- Brown kraft paper is not a reasonable substitute for a release paper since it may adhere to the artwork or platen if any glue residue has been left.

- Release papers cannot be used for predrying because they cannot absorb moisture. Excessive moisture can badly cockle and warp a release paper envelope in addition to affecting the silicone surface.

- Use release boards only on the top of the mounting package to insure a constant, even press against the platen.

- Release boards provide protection against leaving an edge mark on the poster when mounting oversized pieces in the press.

CLEAR RELEASE FILMS

Clear release sheets are generally a polyester film sheet (Mylar or Melinex) coated with silicone or Teflon®. Clear release sheets are often used with glass-top vacuum presses—this allows the operator to see through the glass and through the release film to monitor the mounting process. When mounting high-gloss photographs and prints, the surface of the polyester film provides a very smooth surface. The film may be a bit difficult to work with because it can create static electricity which attracts dust and dirt.

Tapes, Hinges, Mounting Strips, Pockets

All artwork put into a frame must be supported. If the art is just placed in the frame and pressed against the glazing, it will buckle. Although full mounting is the main subject of this book, it is important to understand the basics of other types of attachments. These methods are suitable where full mounting is not appropriate.

Suspension methods used to support art involve hinging to a support board or encasing in edge supports, while allowing the art to expand and contract in response to the environment. There are many methods and materials used for these purposes. Both methods hold artwork in place.

Attaching the art to the back side of the window mat is easiest but should be limited to small artwork. The window opening makes the mat a somewhat weak support.

Attaching the art to the backing board is best as this board is a solid, flat sheet that provides strong support for holding the art in position. Art attached to the backing board can remain undisturbed in the event of future matting replacements. Attaching to the back takes a bit more time to position properly, but it is the preferred method, especially for larger pieces.

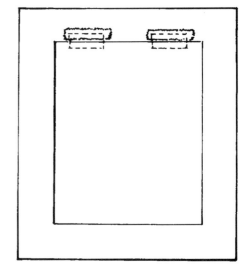

Hinge Attachment

Attachment Methods

Attachment methods include tapes, hinges, and independent supports. Many of these methods relate to conservation techniques. Here is a brief overview of these materials. For a thorough discussion of this topic, see *Volume 4, Conservation Framing.*

Tapes

The choice of adhesive is an important consideration in suspension methods. Polyvinyl tapes such as 3M's #810 tape (Magic Mending) are suitable adhesives for some practical framing jobs, in which the artwork to be framed is of minimal value. These tapes are strong, stable, and clean but are not reversible. Often the carrier sheet can be removed with a solvent, but some of the adhesive will remain on the paper.

Never use cellophane, surgical, filament, brown paper, duct tapes, rubber cement or masking tape. Many of these gum-based adhesives dry out and leave deep stains on the paper. They are not suitable for any purpose in professional picture framing.

Place tape only at the top edge of the artwork. Do not tape all four sides or tape the corners—buckling will result. Double-sided tape, more commonly known as ATG tape, can also be used at the top edge. Be aware that these tapes are permanent. They may also grip very tightly, and if humidity in the frame increases, the paper art may expand at a different rate from the backing board, while the tape holds tight. This will cause buckling of the weakest component—the artwork.

HINGES

Fine quality conservation hinges can be made with cooked rice or wheat starch or methyl cellulose paste applied to torn strips of Japanese paper. Gummed linen/cotton or gummed paper tape may also be used when strength is needed.

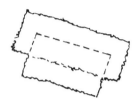

T hinge

Hinges made from pressure-sensitive tapes are permanent; they are not removable with water. Although some of these tapes are clean, stable, and will not discolor, they are permanent and get stronger as they age. Removing the tapes with a solvent will leave residue from the adhesive and the solvent in the art.

INDEPENDENT SUPPORTS

Besides Tapes and Hinges, it is also possible to support artwork with independent attachments, in which no adhesive makes contact with the art.

MOUNTING STRIPS

Mounting Strips are flat supports made from polyester film (Mylar or Melinex) and acid-free rag board with a pressure-sensitive adhesive. They may be cut to size and placed around the edge of a picture. The strips are attached to the backing boards. They provide a small ledge upon which the art sits. Allow space for expansion and contraction.

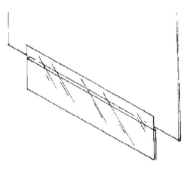

Mounting Strips

CORNER POCKETS

Corner pockets are made from either paper or polyester film and are available in a variety of styles and sizes. They support the artwork only by the corners so they should only be used with small items or in conjunction with mounting strips. Allow space for expansion and contraction.

EDGE STRIPS

Various types of edge supports can be handmade from Japanese or rag papers. See *Volume 4, Conservation Framing*, for instructions for constructing these supports.

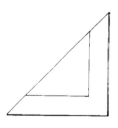

Corner Pockets

Reversing Mounting
Please be careful!

If you are reading this section, you are probably in trouble. Please read the entire section before deciding to use any of these methods. ALL methods are risky.

First, The Disclaimer
Over many years of framing, there have been times when even the most bizarre and risky solution to a problem seems worth a try. But understand clearly that reversing a permanent bond takes skill and practice, even then, haste *will* make waste, and you'll wish you had never started this project. Please practice on something made of similar materials before trying these methods on your client's art.

Reversing with Heat
Some heat-activated adhesives can be removed by reheating the mounted art and gently peeling the artwork from it's mount while still warm. This will only work with removable types of dry mount films and tissues. These are the adhesives which form their bond while cooling. Reheating the adhesive will release the bond until it cools.

This type of un-mounting can be successful with small items where the total item can be removed quickly before the item has a chance to cool and re-bond. On larger items this may not be possible. If the item can withstand greater heat then raise the temperature of your heat press a little. This allows more time to release the print. (Care must be taken not to burn yourself.) One technique is to heat the item in the press and peel back as much of the item as possible before it cools, then slip a piece of double sided release paper between the item and its substrate. This will prevent the freshly freed item from being remounted when it is reheated. This process may have to be repeated several times to completely remove the item. One problem with this technique it that the pressure exerted by the heat press will cause a crease or line at the edge of the release paper each time it is reheated. This may create a problem with thin or glossy papers. To lessen the creasing do not clamp the mechanical press down tight or if using a heat vacuum press reduce the pressure.

Another technique to remove a mounted item with heat is to heat the item in the heat press, remove it and start to peel it back from the substrate. Then roll the item on a print mailing tube while using a heat gun (from a shrink wrap machine) or a hair dryer. Methodically direct the heat across the bonded edge where the rolled underside of the print meets the substrate, while gently rolling the article on the tube. Pressure and heat must be kept even to prevent the item from tearing or stretching. Keep a sheet of release paper on the face of the print while it is being rolled on the tube—this will keep the print from adhering to itself with the warm adhesive residue.

Reversing a bond with heat will probably not work with papers that are thin and weak. The bond could be stronger than the paper and the force needed to remove the item from the adhesive could tear or stretch the paper. Some items are best left to a paper conservator.

Reversing a bond with heat often leaves some adhesive residue on the back of the item which may be difficult to remove. Excess adhesive can be removed with additional heat and rubbing or with solvents (see Reversing With Solvents later in this chapter). If you are going to remount the item and the adhesive residue is evenly distributed over the back, use the same type of adhesive and remount the

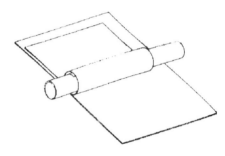

Use a tube to support the print while it is being removed.

item. If the adhesive is in patches or the back is rough, one possible solution may be to use multiple layers of a dry mounting film. Film adhesive melts when heated and will fill in voids creating a smoother bond. If the item can withstand the heat, increase the temperature and time a little to increase the flow of the adhesive and the leveling effect.

Reversing with Water
Adhesives that are water reversible are theoretically ideal, since a bit of clean distilled water should do no harm to most art on paper. However, how much water will be necessary to reverse a full mount? Can the art media be soaked without harm? Moisture will cause the fibers of many types of paper to swell resulting in buckles and wrinkles. Some inks and paints may be water soluble causing them to bleed or wash away. Test before using water to reverse a mount.

REVERSING WITH SOLVENTS

Solvents are dissolving agents. They soften adhesives to allow the separation of a print from the substrate it was mounted to. One advantage of chemicals solvents is, unlike water, they will not cause the paper fibers to swell. However, solvents will dissolve some plastics. <u>Always</u> <u>TEST before using.</u>

In addition to testing the paper and substrate for tolerance of the solvent, test the artwork in spots as well—some inks and other media may be affected by the solvent. Also be aware—any solvent strong enough to soften adhesives is potentially harmful to humans. Use in a well-ventilated area—this is important! Follow manufacturers instructions. Be aware of the solvent's flash point. The flash point is the lowest temperature at which the vapors can ignite if they come in contact with a heat source.

Solvents do not allow the complete removal of adhesive from the item. In fact, they can soften the adhesive and force it further into the paper making it nearly impossible to remove completely. Tough jobs should be left to a paper conservator.

Two solvents marketed to the picture framing industry are UnStik™ and Adhesive Release™. They will dissolve most adhesives used in the industry. Other solvents from the art material and finishing industry include acetone, toluene, and mineral spirits. These like most solvents are potentially harmful to humans and should only be used in a well-ventilated area. Read the manufacturer's instructions and warnings. These solvents are flammable and need to be stored in a safe place. A dispensing can with a valve should be used to minimize the amount used and the user's exposure to the solvent. Remember to test all components of the mounting for compatibility before applying any solvent.

After successfully testing the artwork, use the solvent to loosen a corner of the artwork. While wearing protective gloves, slowly peel the artwork from the substrate while applying solvent to the area still bonded. Use a minimum amount of the solvent. Use steady, even pressure, making sure not to stretch the paper, to prevent it from tearing. Wrap the loosened artwork on a cardboard or plastic tube to keep from poking a finger through the weakened paper. Position the artwork so the solvent will flow toward the still bonded area while keeping the artwork unsaturated and free from dissolved adhesive.

Use a Valvespout® container to control the application of solvents.

While valuable art should be unmounted only by a paper conservator, every framer will one day face the challenge of unmounting a piece they just mounted, to correct a mistake. There are many combinations of items, conditions and materials. There is no one method that will reverse mount everything. Test the item and proceed slowly. Although many mounting techniques are technically reversible, removal can be difficult. It is best to decide before artwork is mounted whether or not bonding it to a substrate will be acceptable over time. Even if the owner of the artwork is not concerned about removing it from its mounting, reversibility can be important to framers, as problems that can emerge during the mounting process (bubbles, wrinkles, etc.) may force the framer to investigate reversing techniques immediately!

SOLVENTS TYPICALLY USED IN PICTURE FRAMING INCLUDE:

ADHESIVE RELEASE. Contains naphtha, a by-product of coal tar distillation. Belongs to the benzol group of solvents. Highly toxic and strong odor. Flash point is below 73°F.

MINERAL SPIRITS. Similar to turpentine, this colorless, volatile solvent is distilled from crude petroleum oils. Mild odor. Flash point is between 100 and 140°F.

ACETONE. Lacquer solvent, principal ingredient in many paint removers. Volatile but relatively low in toxicity. Flash point is 73° F.

TOLUENE. Colorless solvent with a characteristic odor. Can be absorbed through the skin. Flash point is 100°F.

UN-DU® (DOUMAR PRODUCTS.) Solvent marketed to consumers for removal of stickers, labels, price tags and tape. Contains Heptane, which has a very low flash point. Avoid fumes and contact with skin.

Some methods of mounting are truly reversible, some claim to be but really are not, and some are simply not and never will be. To be truly reversible, mounted artwork must be able to be separated from its mounting with no alteration of the artwork. Not only must no remnants of tissue or film remain on the artwork, there must also be no residue of adhesive or solvent. The adhesive carrier is often easy to completely remove; the adhesive itself and lingering solvent residue are the tricky parts.

TERMINOLOGY
FOR MOUNTING PROCESSES

ADHESIVE
A bonding agent, such as glue or paste, designed to join two materials. Mounting adhesives for picture framing may be wet or dry, liquid or solid, independent or attached to a paper or board carrier.

ADHESIVE RELEASE™
Chemical solvent used to remove artwork from its mounting. Separating the art from the mounting may be easy, but some adhesive often remains on the artwork and can be very difficult to remove entirely.

ARCHIVAL
Refers to storage, as in archives; often used to indicate suitability for preservation processes. The term is unregulated, so products called "archival" may or may not meet all the standards of conservation quality.

BRAYER
A rolling cylinder, generally made of hard or soft rubber, attached to a handle for applying paste or exerting pressure.

BURNISHER
A hand tool with hard smooth edges, available in various styles and materials, used in mounting for smoothing or applying pressure to pressure-sensitive adhesives.

COLD MOUNT
Mounting without the use of heat. This term is often used to refer to pressure-sensitive mounting, but could also refer to wet mounting.

COVER SHEET
Protective layer that shields the surface of the artwork during mounting. Frequently a sheet of paper or board coated with a release material that resists the mounting adhesive.

DIAPHRAGM
Also called a bag or bladder. Flexible rubber part of a vacuum press, which molds itself around the substrate, conforming to mounting packages of any depth.

DRY MOUNT
The process of bonding an item to a substrate using pressure and heat-activated adhesives.

DWELL TIME
The amount of time the mounting package remains in the press.

FILM
Heat-activated mounting adhesive in solid form, which melts completely during mounting. Also refers to laminating materials.

HINGE
Hinges are typically made from Japanese papers, but may also be tapes or other materials. They are used to attach artwork to a backing board, using minimal amounts of conservation adhesive.

LAMINATE
To apply a clear polyester or polyvinyl film to the surface of artwork, or encase items between two sheets of film. Matboard manufacturers use the term lamination to refer to the bonding of the layers that create a mat or mount board.

MOUNT
Attachment to a support. In picture framing, mounting methods range from minimal attachment such as conservation hinges, to permanent full attachment of the artwork to a substrate.

MOUNTING PACKAGE
All of the materials for a particular mounting project, stacked together in order.

ORANGE PEEL
A series of small dents on the surface of a mounted high-gloss photograph, caused by texture in the substrate and/or adhesive.

PERFORATOR/PIERCER
A hand tool with small, spiked rolling wheels attached to a handle, for perforating laminating films. Perforating may also be called "piercing."

PERMANENT
Not removable. In mounting, refers to mounting processes that cannot be reversed. Attempting to reverse permanent adhesives requires chemicals and techniques that most often result in damage to art.

pH
The measure of acidity or alkalinity in a substance. The logarithmic scale ranges from 0 (acid) to 14 (alkaline); the neutral point is 7.

PLATEN

The metal or glass underside of the lid on a mounting press, which provides a smooth surface for the mounting package.

POROUS

Containing tiny holes through which moisture and air can move. The porosity of the item that will be mounted, the adhesive used, and the substrate beneath them should all be considered when making mounting decisions.

PREDRY

Predrying removes moisture from materials in the mounting package, especially the artwork and substrate, before proceeding with the mounting. This is done in a heated mechanical press or vacuum press.

PRESSURE-SENSITIVE

Adhesives that adhere on contact and bond under pressure.

RELEASE PAPER

Sheets or rolls of smooth, adhesive-resistant paper or film that protects artwork and mounting presses from unwanted adhesive transfer. May be opaque or clear, single- or double-sided.

RELEASE BOARD

A board coated with an adhesive-resistant paper or film. Used to protect artwork and mounting presses from unwanted adhesive transfer.

SPONGE PAD

A thick, dense sponge foam material with a top layer of felt which rests in the bottom of a mechanical soft-bed dry mount press.

SPONGE SHEET

Soft sponge foam sheet used on the surface of the mounting package to help push or form the mounting process around curves and bevels. Also used for laminating.

SUBSTRATE

The underlying support that artwork is attached to in mounting. Typically a matboard, foam center board, or mounting board, but may be other types of materials.

TACKING

Minimal spot attachment with a hot tacking iron. Used with heat-activated mounting tissues, to hold artwork in position until mounting is completed.

THERMOPRINTING

These printing processes use heat during production, and heat applied to the finished product may adversely affect inks and finishes.

TISSUE

Thin sheets of adhesive-coated paper, activated by heat.

ULTRAVIOLET

The invisible portion of the light spectrum that causes damage to artwork. Using ultraviolet-filtering materials helps minimize the harm.

VACUUM MOUNT

Mounting process that uses the suction of a mechanical vacuum to create pressure. Includes a rubber diaphragm, bladder, or blanket to give flexible support. Vacuum presses may be cold mount only or combination presses that use both heat and cold.

THE WORKROOM

The ideal workroom for mounting would have large flat uncluttered surfaces for assembling the mounting packages. This space would be clean and away from the dust creating areas of the shop. There would be enough space to create an efficient work flow. It may not be practical or possible in most frame shops to create this ideal mounting area but the following considerations should be addressed.

WORK SURFACES

- The work surfaces need to be clean and flat. The area needs to be large enough to assemble the components of the mounting package. The most common mistake in mounting is the mis-alignment of the item, the adhesive or the substrate. This is caused by the slipping of one of the components as it is moved or placed in the press.

- A flat work surface near the press will greatly reduce mis-alignment problems. Balancing boards on top of cutters and other equipment will create problems. Mounting is serious work and requires a designated area for assembling the materials, performing the work and allowing mounted items to cool.

- A mechanical heat press needs open areas on both sides to accommodate large sheets. Presses are too heavy to move whenever extra room is needed. An advantage of a mechanical press is the mounting of large items by taking multiple bites, but this works only if the area is free of obstructions.

- COOLING TABLE AND WEIGHT
  A cooling table and weight may seem to be a frivolous item, but when the mounting process requires a cooling period outside of the press the space is mandatory. Setting a wet or warm mounted poster on top of a worktable with tools and mat cutters will result in a warped piece. The top of the hot vacuum press is not a good cooling area because of the residual heat from the press.

DUST CONTROL

If at all possible keep the mounting supplies and work area away from the dust producing areas of the shop. A small speck of dust will look like a mountain under a glossy print. Good lighting will reveal these dust particles before it is too late.

Dry mount table with horizontal storage for boards and roll storage for tissues on the side. Instructions for building this table can be found in
How to Build Frameshop Worktables, Fixtures & Jigs
by Paul MacFarland.

ORGANIZED STORAGE OF MATERIALS

Ideally everything is at hand, but often frame shops are cramped for space and keeping everything close is not an option. Look at the space above the press for storage of adhesives. Perhaps shelving or racks suspended from the ceiling could improve accessibility. In a low volume shop the rolls of adhesive should be stored in their box to keep from getting dusty.

STORAGE

While it is preferable to store mat and mount boards flat it is often not practical. If boards must be stored on edge it is best to keep them in their original packaging and in narrow bins to reduce warping. The area should be dry with low humidity.

Rolls of adhesive can be hung on rods suspended from a shelf or ceiling. Label the rolls, to avoid confusion—it is possible to confuse release paper with some mounting tissue. The identifying label can also have the operating temperature and other helpful instructions. Boxes of adhesive in sheet form should be stored flat and, like other adhesives, in a cool area.

ADEQUATE LIGHTING

Since dust particles and stray pieces of film, even notes, work orders and razor blades, have been known to creep into the mounting package before it goes into a press, good lighting is necessary for identifying unwanted items in the mounting package.

WORK FLOW

The work flow in the mounting area is very important. The ideal setup allows the work to move smoothly from the set-up area (where the mounting package is assembled) to the press. From the press the newly mounted item is moved to a separate cooling area, ideally next to the press. Moving large boards in a crowded frame shop is not easy but with a little planning the mounting area can be an efficient work area.

PLACEMENT AND HEIGHT OF EQUIPMENT

- Access to the equipment is a major concern, especially when large pieces are being processed. Is there room on both sides of the press? If you are using a mechanical press, the sides are very important for feeding large sheets for multiple "bites."

- The height of the equipment is just as important in the mounting area as in the rest of the workroom. The mechanical heat press needs to be placed at a height where the clamping handle can be reached and pulled shut without great effort.

CHAPTER 2

DRY MOUNTING

Dry mounting is "dry" because the adhesives used with this method are supplied in dry, solid form, in sheets or rolls or adhered to boards. They provide a complete, even layer of adhesive, along with ease of handling. Dry mounting might also be called "heat mounting," because dry mounting adhesives are activated by heat.

Dry mounting adhesives are either tissues or films. The tissues are a thin paper layer completely coated with adhesive; they are stable and do not migrate. The films are solid adhesive that will melt and flow into a bonding layer.

Many papers and media will easily tolerate the levels of heat used in dry mounting with no alteration except the desired one—bonding to the substrate. But the application of heat to artwork requires caution, because materials may react in unpredictable ways. Testing before mounting is recommended whenever possible.

TIME
The mounting package must remain in the press long enough to activate the adhesive and create the bond to the substrate. For adhesives that bond while cooling, the package must be removed from the press and immediately put under weights until completely cool.

TEMPERATURE
The temperature of the press should be guided by the heat requirements of the adhesive. The adhesive choice is determined by the characteristics of the art being mounted. Press temperature should be calibrated and occasionally rechecked for accuracy.

PRESSURE
In dry mounting, pressure is applied with the weight of a platen or the suction of a vacuum. Since a machine will control the pressure placed on the artwork, it is important to properly set and adjust the machine.

MOISTURE
Moisture trapped in the substrate or artwork expands when heated and, if not released from the mounting package, will cause incomplete bonds and bubbles. This problem is made greater with the use of non-porous items which do not allow the moisture to escape. Predrying the substrate and artwork will help eliminate this risk.

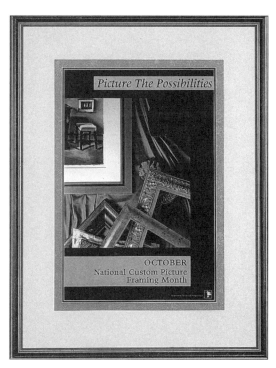

Posters are the most popular mounting jobs.

EQUIPMENT

MECHANICAL PRESSES

A mechanical press uses a leveraged clamping action to apply pressure to the artwork and the substrate. Up to 4 lbs. of pressure is applied. The top platen is heated and is controlled by a thermostat. Two types of mechanical presses are available: soft bed and hard bed. A soft bed press has a hard metal top plate which heats, and a dense sponge pad at the bottom of the bed. The hard bed press has metal plates for both top and bottom; the top plate is heated. Hard bed presses are excellent for mounting to wood and wood-like substrates.

Bienfang's Masterpiece 550 Soft Bed Press

FEATURES OF A MECHANICAL PRESS:
- Heat mounts, cold mounts and laminates
- Single mounts up to platen size
- Artwork which is larger than the press itself can be mounted using a multiple-bite process
- Takes up less physical tabletop space than a vacuum press
- Some models use standard 110-volt electrical outlet
- Can be used in conjunction with tissues, paste, pressure-sensitive, and spray adhesives
- Fast mounting time
- Can be adjusted for different substrate thicknesses
- Mounting materials may have to be predried
- Several sizes available from 15x18" to 26x34"

Drytac Hard Bed Press

Vacuum Press & Frame Systems

A vacuum press, instead of using mechanical forces to apply pressure, uses the weight of air pressure. Using a vacuum pump, air is evacuated (or sucked) from between a rigid surface and a flexible bladder or rubber blanket. The difference in air pressure between the inside and outside can result in a force of up to 12 lbs. per square inch.

The two types of systems are:
1. Cold vacuum presses provide pressure and remove moisture from boards and adhesives. Can be used with wet pastes and spray adhesives.

2. The Hot/Cold Combination Press provides the pressure of a vacuum and the option of heat. The surface platen which may be see-through glass or a metal sheet, is heated.

Features of a Combination Hot/Cold Vacuum Press
- Heat mounts, cold mounts, laminates
- Automatically adjusts to substrate thickness
- Pulls moisture from materials
- Several pieces may be mounted at the same time
- Most dry mounting adhesives may be used
- Maximum size of mounting limited to size of the press frame
- No oversized, multiple-bite capabilities
- Monitoring of vacuum pump, filter, oil on some models
- Requires 220-volt, three or four-wire hook-up
- Higher electrical usage than a mechanical press
- Mounting time is longer than a mechanical press
- Several sizes available, from 21x25" to 56x103"

The Bienfang Vacuum Press 4468H

Electronic control key pads are available on many brands of presses.

Hot Press HGP 260 Vacuum Press

TACKING IRON

A tacking iron is used to lightly melt a small area of dry mount adhesive to the art and the substrate. This positions the items to be mounted onto the substrate so they do not shift as they are moved into the press or during the mounting process.

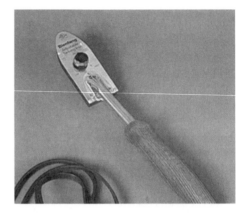

WEIGHTS

Weights should be used on top of a mounting package while it is cooling. They are very important to the lasting flatness of a mounted item. Flat metal weights with lift handles are available from suppliers or a sheet of 1/4" plate glass can be used. This glass should be large enough to accommodate most of the anticipated mountings, but still small enough to handle. Glass in an excellent weight because it is heat-absorbent, transparent and may be used as a cutting surface. Suction-grip handles are available for lifting and moving glass weights.

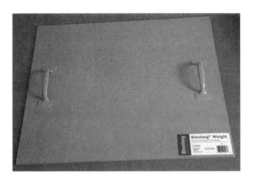

PERFORATOR

A perforating tool has several wheels with sharp points, used to pierce laminating film for certain types of lamination.

KRAFT PAPER

Simple brown kraft paper, used in many frame shops as dust covers, can be used as a protective sheet in several mounting processes. It can be folded to make a protective envelope to hold the work, adhesive and substrate as it goes into the press. It is smooth, absorbent and relatively inexpensive.

DUSTING BRUSH

A dusting brush has long, narrow rows of bristles on a handle for easy control. Available with soft or stiff hairs, natural or synthetic bristles, this provides a gentle, wide band of dusting that can be swept across the surface of mounting boards and most artwork.

PLATEN CLEANER

A paste compound that removes adhesive residue and foreign material from press platens.

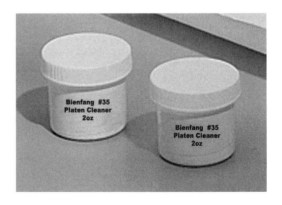

ADHESIVES

Choosing the right bonding agent is very important for successful mounting. Manufacturer specifications are usually clear about the composition, the heat range and the suggested uses.

There are several categories of dry mounting adhesives. Tissue or film, porous or non-porous, permanent or removable.

Dry mounting tissues are a thin paper layer completely coated with adhesive; they are stable and do not migrate. They may be acid-free They are easy to handle, have high heat tolerances and are fast setting. Tissues may be porous or non-porous. Porous tissues allow air and moisture to move out of the mounting package, reducing the risk of blisters.

Dry mounting films are solid sheets of adhesive that melt in the heat press but solidify and bond while cooling. They may be acid-free.

Most permanent adhesives bond while heated in the press; the bond is complete once the required dwell time (at the required temperature) has elapsed. The bond is intended to be permanent, meaning removal from the substrate without damage to the art is very unlikely.

Removable adhesives are activated by heat but bond as they cool. Once heated to the correct temperature in the press, the mounting package is removed from the press and immediately put under the pressure of a weight. The adhesive bond completes during cooling. The adhesive is theoretically reversible, meaning the bond between the artwork and the substrate may be broken by reheating the mounted work and carefully separating the two items. With most products, this is not as easy as it sounds. See page 16 for directions and risks.

TISSUE SHEETS VS. TISSUE-COVERED BOARDS
Is it better to buy adhesive and boards separately, or already bonded to one another? For greatest flexibility, the "a la carte" system offers many more options to mix and match substrates and adhesives. However, using boards coated with heat-activated adhesive can be quick and easy, ensuring a flat, unwrinkled adhesive layer. They are also good for fast production mounting of porous papers such as posters. Coated boards are typically priced to echo individual purchasing of adhesive plus mount board, so the cost of both methods is usually about the same. For large scale production, or for shops that deal with a limited range of type and size of artwork, the boards may be time and cost effective.

TISSUE VS. FILM
Dry mounting tissues are thin paper layers coated with adhesive; they are stable, meaning they do not migrate when heated. Films are solid sheets of adhesive that melt when heated; they can be layered or pieced because the adhesive levels as it melts.

POROUS VS. NON-POROUS
A porous material allows air and moisture to pass through; a non-porous material does not. Artwork, substrates and mounting adhesives may be porous or non-porous. It is important that some elements of the mounting package be porous to allow air and moisture to find a path out of the package.

PERMANENT VS. REMOVABLE
Most permanent dry mounting adhesives bond in the press while hot. Removable tissues and films are heat-activated but bond as they cool. Cooling under a weight facilitates the bond.

ACID-FREE
Mounting adhesives that are described as acid-free are either naturally inert or treated with a buffering agent.

DRY MOUNT ADHESIVES
TISSUES & FILMS

BUFFERMOUNT™ (BIENFANG)
Acid-free adhesive with a buffered paper core and very low bonding temperature (160°-190°F). It is especially designed for use with high-quality art, photos and very thin, delicate materials such as rice paper, tissue and silk. Removable.

CLEARMOUNT® (BIENFANG)
This adhesive was specially formulated for mounting pigment inkjet reproductions of artwork and photographs without the risk of future discoloration. Clear film that creates a permanent bond at a low temperature (190°F.)

COLORMOUNT® (BIENFANG)
Permanent, porous, low temperature (175°-200°F) tissue that works well with resin-coated photos, slick glossy papers and regular papers. Versatile, works well with many papers and substrates.

FUSION 4000® (BIENFANG)
Ultra-clear, acid-free, pure adhesive film that works well with textured surfaces, fabrics and large pieces done in sections because it melts smoothly, evenly and completely during heating (160°F). It bonds while it cools. Removable when reheated.

PROMOUNT (PRINT MOUNT)
Breathable, neutral pH tissue. Permanent, bonds at low temperature (180°F.) Very versatile. Good bond with plastic coated photo papers including RC and Cibachrome. Mounts to a wide variety of substrates.

ECONOMOUNT (PRINT MOUNT)
Practical mounting tissue for all general dry mounting applications. Activates at 175°F, can be removed at 210°F. Suitable for mounting on matboard, foam board, and mounting boards. Not recommended for mounting on Masonite.

SAFEMOUNT (PRINT MOUNT)
Buffered paper tissue coated on both sides with heat-reversible adhesive. Recommended temperature 175°F. Designed for use with fine art photographs, prints, silk, and rice papers.

VERSAMOUNT (PRINT MOUNT)
100% pure adhesive film that activates at a low temperature (160°F) and bonds while cooling. Removable by reheating. Melts completely when heated, so it can be used for mounting fabric and textured artwork.

TECHMOUNT
Porous tissue which is coated on both sides with a heat-activated, low temperature (160°-170°F), permanent adhesive. Use with RC photos, smooth paper art, posters, clay-coated papers, newspapers and cotton and polyester fabrics.

DRYCHIVAL™ (DRYTAC)
Acid-free, permanent, very low temperature (160°F) adhesive on a buffered tissue. Ideal for photos, paper, prints, and delicate items that require low temperatures.

DRY MOUNT FILM (DRYTAC)
A permanent, double-sided thermoset PVC film coated on both sides with protective release paper. Low initial tack adhesive allows positioning of a print without the use of a tacking iron. Adhesive activates at 175°F. Can use with non-porous or textured items.

TRIMOUNT™ (DRYTAC)
Porous, permanent, low temperature (175°F) all-purpose tissue. Suitable for most applications but ideal for RC photos. Neutral pH.

FLOBOND™ (DRYTAC)
Pure, clear, removable, pH neutral, low temperature (175°F) film adhesive. Mounts prints, posters, parchment, and foils to a variety of substrates including matboards, foam center boards, and some metals. Use to mount fabrics, coarse papers and other irregular materials.

GICLÉEMOUNT™ (DRYTAC)
Colorless, non-yellowing mounting film designed specifically for mounting giclées and photo papers. Permanent, with a temperature range of 190°F-225°F.

VISTAMOUNT™ (DRYTAC)
General purpose dry mounting tissue with buffered white carrier. Activates at low temperature (170°F.) White carrier prevents showthrough when mounting thin paper to dark substrates.

GENERAL PURPOSE MOUNTING TISSUE (UNITED)
Economy brand glassine, permanent.

CLEARBOND 2000 (UNITED)
Economy brand removable film comparable.

SUPERMOUNT (UNITED)
Economy brand porous, permanent tissue.

DRY MOUNTING ADHESIVES MOUNTED TO BOARDS

Some dry mounting adhesives are available precoated on foam board for quick and easy mounting.

SINGLESTEP® (BIENFANG)

Adhesive on one side of a smooth 3/16" foam board forms a smooth, permanent bond at 180°F. SINGLESTEP PLUS® activates at a low 160°F so it can be used with photographs and other low temperature items. Available white or all black.

SPEEDMOUNT® (NIELSEN BAINBRIDGE)

Low temperature pH neutral adhesive on a smooth foam board, 1/8" or 3/16" thick. Temperature range 150°F-190°F.

ARTCARE RESTORE® (NIELSEN BAINBRIDGE)

Reversible, low temperature adhesive on Artcare® foam board. Activates at 150°F-160°F with a dwell time of 15-30 seconds.

HEAT-ACTIVATED FOME-COR® (CRESCENT)

Low temperature adhesive on 1/8" or 3/16" foam board.

Names of tissues and films may change as companies introduce new products, discontinue products or change the names of products.

The names of companies may also change as the companies are bought, sold, or expanded.

New products are introduced regularly. To evaluate a new dry mounting adhesive, consider all of the key attributes: temperature range, porosity (breathability), permanence, buffering, etc.

Dry mounting tissues and films are typically sold in rolls..

BASIC DRY MOUNTING PROCEDURE

The basic steps are consistent for most dry mounting projects, but the specifics will vary with the type of press used, and the materials selected.

1. Test a small corner of the artwork for heat sensitivity if there is any doubt about its ability to tolerate heat. Tacking irons can be very hot. If planning to use a low temperature mounting adhesive, do not use the tacking iron for your test.

2. Select a substrate and adhesive appropriate for the artwork to be mounted.

3. Set the press to the appropriate temperature for the selected adhesive and allow it to heat.

4. Predry the art and substrate by placing each in the press for a short time, such as 15 -30 seconds, depending on thickness of materials and humidity level of the air.

5. Lay the substrate on a flat surface. Make sure the substrate surface is free of dust and particles. Place the adhesive tissue or film on top of the substrate.

6. Place the artwork face up on the adhesive layer. Trim excess adhesive (it could fold over onto the artwork during the mounting process).

7. Tack the art in place with a tacking iron, placing a small piece of release paper over the spot where the tacking iron will touch the art. Tack at the edge of one corner. Do not tack all along one side, all four corners, an "x" in the middle, etc. This will restrict the artwork and adhesive from moving against the substrate as necessary during mounting. The tack is only meant to hold the art in place so it doesn't shift while moving to the press.

8. Put the substrate, adhesive, and art into the press. Use a sheet of release paper sufficient to cover the substrate, to keep the press clean. Make sure the entire package is flat and wrinkle-free.

9. Close the press. Allow the appropriate dwell time.

10. Remove the unit from the press. For adhesives that bond while cooling and for stubborn or resistant pieces, cool under weight immediately upon removal from the press. Weights may be metal plates or 1/4" thick plate glass with smoothed edges.

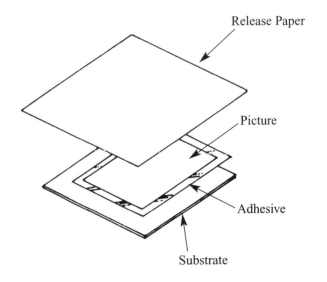

Release Paper

Picture

Adhesive

Substrate

Tacking on edge with a small piece of release paper.

TACKING

Tacking irons are used to apply heat to a small area on the mounting package. This is used to hold the elements of the package together as they go into the press, thus preventing slipping and shifting. Always use a scrap of release paper between the art and the tacking iron.

Tack only on the end or edge of the package.

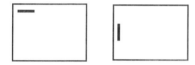

Do not tack on all four corners or in the middle. This would restrict the materials from expanding and contracting with the heating and cooling process.

An alternative tacking method is the "z" tack. With this method, the artwork is placed face down with the adhesive layer on top of it. Using a small piece of release paper where the tacking iron will touch, tack in one small spot at one edge of the artwork. Place the artwork face up on the substrate. Gently lift the tacked end of the artwork, leaving the adhesive layer in contact with the substrate. Using release paper where the tacking iron will touch, tack the adhesive to the substrate in one spot along the edge.

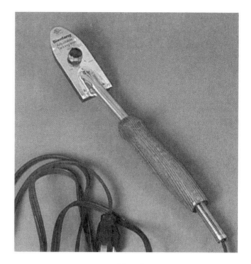

tacking iron

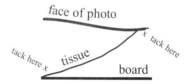

The "Z" tacking method: tack the tissue to the back side of the photo and the top side of the mounting board.

Dry Mounting Tips

- Test mount as many different types of artwork as possible using various adhesives that are stocked in the frame shop. This "presolving" of problems protects customer artwork.

- Make small samples of mounting disasters, to show customers what would happen if the framer agreed to dry mount their thermoprinted baseball tickets, their Ilfochrome Classic photo, or their skin document.

- Make samples to help sell mounting. Show customers unmounted paper art that has buckled and slumped in a frame. "Half-mount" a wrinkled print, to show the difference between the mounted and unmounted halves. Make a mounted collage of photos to spark customer interest—customers often don't realize how nice these can look when professionally mounted.

- Use a portable dehumidifier if necessary to control moisture in the workshop, especially in humid climates. Remember to empty the reservoir! (Or attach a drain hose.)

- For mechanical presses, check the platen regularly for cleanliness.

- For vacuum presses, make sure nothing obstructs the secure closing of the lid. The edge must be completely free of stray pieces of paper, etc. or the vacuum may not draw properly.

Adjusting Temperature of the Press

Use Temperature Indicator Strips to check the temperature of the press. These special strips have two wax indicators which have a specific melting point. One indicator melts at 200°F and the other at 210°F.

1. Turn on press and set thermostat for 200°F.

2. After press has cycled at least once, place an indicator strip inside one of the folded pieces of release paper that is supplied with the strips.

3. Assemble the mounting package in the following order:
   top release paper
   release paper/indicator unit
   substrate
   bottom release paper

4. After leaving package in press for normal dwell time, take the package out of the press and examine the indicator strip. The 200°F indicator strip should be melted and the 210°F indicator strip should not. If this did not happen, continue with the following steps.

5. Note where the thermostat and thermometer are with a pencil line. Make an adjustment to the thermostat and repeat process.

6. Once you have found the correct position for the 200°F, mark both the thermostat and thermometer. If the press allows calibration for the thermostat and thermometer, make the necessary adjustments. If not, note where the true 200°F is and determine the other temperatures.

Robert Mayfield, CPF, GCF

LAMINATING

Lamination is used to apply a clear polyester, polyvinyl film or acetate film to the surface of artwork, or encase items between two sheets of film. The different types have different technical requirements.

Laminating films may have a textured surface or a gloss or matte finish. They are available perforated/pierced or as a solid sheet. Pierced polyvinyl films allows air and moisture to pass through the film during the mounting process. This is important with artwork such as RC photos, which are non-porous. During the mounting process, trapped air must have a path to exit or air bubbles will be created.

The holes are very tiny and will melt shut during the heating process. Only PVC films should be perforated, because holes made in polyester or acetate films will not self-seal when heated.

USES FOR LAMINATION
Lamination seals the surface of the art; it is not removable. The plastic film melts onto the paper item, so it is permanent.

LAMINATION FOR ART
Lamination is often used to protect a poster or reproduction when glass is inappropriate. It is especially useful for protecting moisture-sensitive paper. Many early giclées were protected with a laminate to protect the delicate ink jet printed surface. Special texturing laminates are made that soften to accept the imprint of a textured overlayer, so the art can be given a variety of surface textures.

LAMINATION FOR NOTE BOARDS
Some laminating films can accept markers so they can be used to make note boards. Be sure to test the laminate for marker removal. The "dry erase" variety is usually appropriate. When making a note board, a hard, smooth substrate is important. If the board will have to accept push pins, then foam core is appropriate. Most foam boards will dent under pressure so an extra-dense foam board is recommended for this purpose.

LAMINATION FOR MAPS
Lamination can be used to encapsulate a print or mat that must be handled repeatedly.

BASIC LAMINATING PROCEDURE

1. Select laminating film. Cut a piece slightly larger than the art being laminated. Perforate if necessary.

2. Peel back a corner of the film's release paper, creasing the paper to keep the film exposed. Attach the exposed corner to the appropriate corner of the art and hold in place with one hand. Use the other hand to pull on the release paper, guiding the exposed film over the surface of the art. The film can be lifted and replaced to allow removal of particles trapped during this procedure. Then smooth the film to release trapped air.

3. If the art is not already dry mounted to a substrate, lay it on a release paper covered board. A surface cover should be set on top of this package. This cover is generally a foam sheet, but may be a foil sheet if high gloss is the goal.

4. Place the package in the press for time recommended by the laminating film manufacturer.

TEMPERATURES FOR LAMINATION
Each film has a suggested temperature, but the choice of temperature for a lamination project must be based on several things:
  a. the film's melting temperature
  b. maximum heat the art will tolerate
  c. maximum heat the substrate will tolerate
  d. the amount of dwell time in the press

If a high temperature cannot be used, a longer dwell time will often compensate.

Laminating Adhesives

Finish Guard-UV (Bienfang)
Vinyl-based film featuring UV inhibitors. Applies at a low temperature of 185°F. May be used on photos, posters and other graphics. Available pre-pierced or unpierced. Available in standard gloss, lustre, satin-matte, ultra-matte, canvas and linen textures.

Texturing Film (Bienfang)
Film that allows versatile custom surface texturing while providing overlaminate protection. Provides UV protection. Available in matte or gloss finishes. Bonds at 200°F-225°F.

ArtShield UV (Drytac)
A thin, clear, 2 mil, low temperature (185°F) PVC film. UV inhibitors are incorporated for protection. Ideal for RC photos and canvas transfers. Available perforated or non-perforated in several finishes.

ArtShield Canvastex (Drytac)
Perforated PVC laminate that adds a fine canvas-grain finish to prints and posters. Emerytex provides a "scuff" resistant, semi-matte, pebble finish. Good for display in high traffic areas or items that are extensively handled.

FlowTex™ Texturing System (Drytac)
Laminate and add surface texture at the same time. The film softens when heated to accept texture from an overlay of fabric or other material. Application temperature 190°F-225°F.

Laminac-UV (Print Mount)
Pre-pierced PVC laminate film available in seven finishes.

Laminac-UV Polyester High Gloss (Print Mount)
Produces a solid, high-gloss surface. Suitable for making write on/wipe off noteboards.

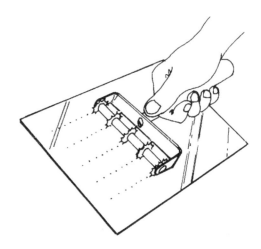

PERFORATOR
A hand tool with small, spiked rolling wheels attached to a handle, for perforating/piercing laminating films.

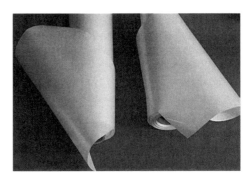

Laminating films typically come in rolls.

CHAPTER 3
WET MOUNTING

Wet mounting is the oldest method of permanently adhering paper or fabric to a substrate (backing board.) Wet mounting uses wet glues and pastes, an applicator for the paste and a weight to apply pressure while it dries. A simple method done with minimum supplies—but it can be messy. Oversized items can be mounted (it may take two people to accomplish) when regular press equipment is not large enough.

Wet mounting in combination with a vacuum press is very fast and effective. Many fabrics can be wet mounted. Fabrics of medium weight work best; sheer or lightweight fabrics such as silk require an experienced hand to avoid adhesive bleedthrough. Wet mounting can be used on paper items such as photographs, posters, reproductions and decorative papers.

The principle of wet mounting is simple: apply paste to a substrate, dampen the paper that will be mounted (this expands the paper fibers), put the two together, apply pressure and wait for the moisture in the paste to evaporate, creating the bond. Note: if mounting fabric, do not dampen the fabric.

The success of permanent mounting is directly related to:
- Application of an even layer of adhesive
- Adequate weight or pressure during drying
- Allowing for appropriate dwell time

Use of a vacuum frame will increase the permanency by creating a stronger bond in a shorter period of time, because it quickly eliminates moisture while applying strong pressure.

A lite of glass the same size as the worktable will make a very effective weight. It will apply even pressure and its top surface can be used as a cutting table.

Temperature becomes an issue when attempting to apply wet adhesives in an extremely hot, humid or cold environment which might affect the flow and/or drying time of the selected adhesive.

TIME
Time required for the evaporation of the pastes depends on the thickness of the adhesive layer, humidity of the environment, use of a press, and whether the item and substrate are absorbent. Time may range from 1 to 24 hours.

MOISTURE
A critical element in the beginning of the process but must be eliminated by the end. A vacuum press will speed up the drying process by quickly removing moisture from the mounting elements.

PRESSURE
Even, consistent pressure is very important. Keeping the materials completely flat (while drying) under a sufficient weight is also important.

TEMPERATURE
Extreme temperatures affect the paste consistency.

Equipment

Cold Vacuum Frame

A cold vacuum frame is the same as the combination hot/cold press without the heating elements. It provides the pressure and remove most moisture from the boards and adhesives without the use of heat. They are used with spray glues, wet pastes and pressure-sensitive adhesives. Pressure is controlled by a rubber bladder being pressed up against the mounting project.

FEATURES OF A COLD VACUUM PRESS:
- Automatically adjusts to substrate thickness
- Automatically pulls most moisture from materials
- Multiple mounting capabilities
- Use with wet, spray and pressure-sensitive adhesive No heat mounting or laminating capabilities
- Maximum mounting limited to press frame size. No oversized, or multiple-bite capabilities
- Maintenance of vacuum pump, filter, oil levels required on some models

The size and structure of a cold vacuum press is the same as a heat vacuum press. Without the ability to heat materials, mounting is limited to wet and spray processes.

Wet Paste Applicators

Paste can be applied with a brush, roller, brayer or spray gun.

Brayer

A brayer is used to apply pressure or to roll-on wet pastes. They are available in several sizes and in rubber or acrylic.

Weights

If using heat in mounting, weights should be used on top of the mounting package while it is cooling. If not using heat, weights are still to the flatness of a mounted item. Heavy flat metal weights with lift handles are available from suppliers. The size is limited and it usually will require two or three of these weights to cover a poster while it is drying.

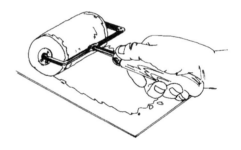

Using a roller to apply wet paste.

A sheet of 1/4" plate glass makes a good weight. This glass should be large enough to accommodate most of the anticipated mountings, or cut it to the size of a worktable. Have the edges ground smooth or apply tape to cover raw glass edges. Suction handles can be used to lift the glass if it is heavy. Glass in a practical weight because it is heat absorbent, transparent and mounted work may be beneath the glass while the surface is used to work on another project.

Kraft Paper

Simple brown kraft paper, used in many frame shops for dust covers, can be used as a protective sheet in several mounting processes. It can be folded to make a protective envelope to hold the artwork, adhesive and substrate as it goes into the press. It is smooth, absorbent and relatively inexpensive.

ADHESIVES

WET GLUES AND PASTES

The following adhesives may be used for wet mounting purposes. Wet glues and pastes must evaporate to become bonded. Evaporation of glues and pastes takes place:

- over time under pressure
- in a vacuum press with or without heat
- in a mechanical press, with or without heat

VACUGLUE 300® (BIENFANG)

Natural vegetable starch-based adhesive that is pH neutral (acid-free), water-soluble, reversible, and odorless. It bonds papers, photos and fabrics to a variety of substrates. It sets quickly in a hot or cold vacuum press, mechanical press or with a rubber brayer. From the bottle it may be applied with a brush, roller or spray gun.

SURE MOUNT ALL-PURPOSE® (PRINTMOUNT)

Water-soluble, acid free, reversible vegetable starch adhesive. Use for paper, photos, fabric, chipboard, foam center board, wood masonite, etc. Will not crack, become brittle or yellow. May be applied with a roller, brush, trowel or spray gun.

YES PASTE® (GANE)

A thick white dextrin-based paste which may be diluted slightly with warm water to achieve desired consistency. Use for wet mounting of papers, leather, polyester to paper, wood, tin, glass and metals. Acid-free.

LAMIN-ALL® (MCDONALD PHOTO PRODUCTS)

Acid-free acrylic polymer adhesive for hot or cold bonding to a wide variety of substrates. May be applied with brush, roller or spray gun.

OTHER PASTES TO CONSIDER:

- Cooked rice starch, wheat starch, or methyl cellulose paste (the same pastes used for conservation hinging.)
- Metlyn® sold in art supply stores for making paper mâché. It is a clear adhesive, a modern version of wallpaper pastes.
- Lineco® Neutral pH white glue.

TIPS

1. Irregular shapes can be applied to a backing by coating the back of the shape from the center outward. Blot with a paper towel then apply to the background.
2. If a mounting board is thin, counter mount by attaching a sheet of plain kraft paper to the back side. It will even out the tension caused by wet pastes expanding and contracting the fibers of the mount board.
3. Apply too much glue? Gently set a sheet of kraft paper over the project to pick up the glue, lift the pick-up sheet from the center—this will pull the paste away from the edges so it won't seep onto the image.
4. Use a 4" wide mohair roller for best coverage of paste.

by Steve Albin

THE BASIC WET MOUNTING PROCESS

MATERIALS:

    Scrap of glass
    Roller, brayer (brush for thin glues)
    Paste
    Weight
    Substrate

1. Pour the paste on the glass, then roll the brayer back and forth to spread the adhesive into an even layer. Do not use a piece of matboard to hold the paste—it will absorb the water in the paste and make the paste dry too quickly.

2. Use a damp sponge or mist the back of the print with water to expand the fibers of the paper.

3 Apply the paste to the substrate. The application should be as even as possible. If it is too thick the print will dent on the surface—too thin and it will dry before the print is set in place. The entire surface must be covered with the paste.

4. Carefully position the damp print onto the pasted area of the substrate. Use a cover sheet to protect the face of the print. Smooth the print in place using a brayer or soft brush. The human hand is not as smooth as a brayer; it may leave finger indentations.

5. Set print under a lite of glass to dry or put into a vacuum press.

TO WET MOUNT A PIECE IN THE CENTER OF A MATBOARD

1. Set the print, face down, on a clean sheet of paper larger than the print.
2. Apply moisture to the back of the print with a mister.
3. Apply paste to print from the center outward towards the edges.
4. Blot with a paper towel to remove excess paste if necessary.
5. Apply the pasted article onto the mount board. Use a cover sheet to protect the face of the print. Smooth in place with a brayer or soft brush.
6. Set a release paper on the face of the mounted item and set aside to dry or put into a vacuum press to complete the mounting.

CHAPTER 4

PRESSURE-SENSITIVE MOUNTING

Pressure-sensitive adhesives bond with pressure. They are typically coated with release papers which protect the adhesives from bonding until needed.

Pressure-sensitive adhesives may be the simplest and cleanest method of mounting paper to a substrate. Since there is no heat involved, there is less chance of melting or other heat-related damage to heat-sensitive images being produced from computers, printers and related technology.

Equipment may be as simple as a brayer and a lite of glass as a weight. Using a press will increase pressure, reduce moisture and provide even pressure quickly

EQUIPMENT

COLD VACUUM FRAMES

The cold vacuum press provides pressure within a vacuum frame without heating elements. The cold vacuum will remove most moisture from the boards and adhesives, while providing even pressure to create the bond.

Cold vacuum presses are used with spray glues, wet pastes and pressure-sensitive adhesives. Pressure is controlled by the rubber bladder being pressed up against the mounting project.

FEATURES OF COLD MOUNT PRESSES:
- Automatically adjusts to substrate thickness
- Automatically pulls most moisture from materials
- Several pieces may be put into the press at one time
- Use with wet, spray and pressure-sensitive adhesive
- Maximum mounting limited to press frame size—no oversized, multiple-bite capabilities
- Monitoring of vacuum pump, filter, oil levels on some models
- Will not mount heat-activated laminates or tissues
- Up to 12 lbs. per square inch of pressure

TIME & TEMPERATURE
Time and temperature are closely related when mounting with pressure-sensitives. The colder the adhesive, the slower the bond. The warmer the adhesive the quicker the bond.

PRESSURE
Pressure creates the bond.

MOISTURE
Moisture will prevent a good bond.

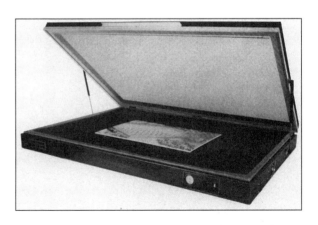

BURNISHER

A burnisher, typically made of plastic, is used to apply pressure to pressure-sensitive adhesives.

BRAYER

A brayer is used to apply pressure or to roll-on wet pastes. They are available in several sizes and in soft or hard rubber.

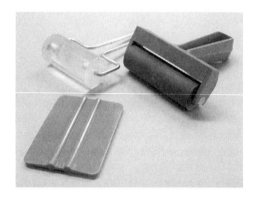

KRAFT PAPER

Simple brown kraft paper, used in many frame shops as dust covers, can be used as a protective sheet in several mounting processes. It can be folded to make a protective envelope to hold the work, adhesive and substrate as it goes into the press. It is smooth, absorbent and relatively inexpensive.

WEIGHTS

A lite of glass with edges taped can be used as a weight while the bond is forming on repositionable pressure-sensitive adhesives.

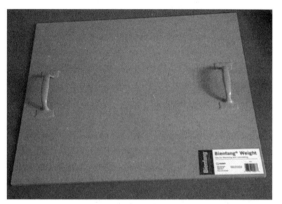

COLD MOUNT MACHINE

A simple hand crank style press. These machines mount and laminate by forcing air from between materials, creating a bond with pressure. The pressure is adjustable and can accommodate different thicknesses depending on the brand of press. Can be used with pressure-sensitive mounting and laminating materials, not heat activated materials.

FEATURES OF CRANK STYLE PRESSES:
- Can laminate and mount with pressure-sensitive adhesives and laminating films
- Takes a small amount of space
- Mounting is limited to the width size of the press
- Can not be used with heat-activated adhesives

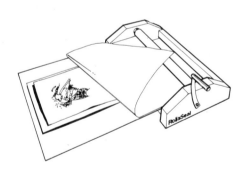

PRESSURE-SENSITIVE FILMS

Pressure-sensitive films can be used to mount pictures with or without a press. They can be used to bond several different types of materials together.

PERFECT MOUNT FILM™ (CRESCENT)
A sheet of adhesive with release paper on both sides. Repositionable, pH neutral, acrylic, clear, non-staining adhesive. The very dry-to-the-touch-adhesive allows for repositioning of paper-based items or fabric. The long open time for repositioning is countered with a long time in setting a permanent bond. It may take from 8 to 24 hours for a permanent bond.

PMA™ (3M)
A repositionable film of adhesive dispensed from a roll. Bond is made permanent with pressure from a hand squeegee, brayer or roller press. Adhesive sets-up quickly. Can be used in conjunction with pressure laminating.

BOARDS
PERFECT MOUNT BOARD™ (CRESCENT)
Repositionable, pH neutral, acrylic, clear, non-staining adhesive on single-thick, double-thick and foam center board. Ideal for photos, paper-based items or fabric. It is repositionable until pressure is applied and then the adhesive becomes a permanent bond.

SUPERSMOOTH™ (CRESCENT)
Ultra-smooth, brilliant white, durable, acid-free, non-yellowing surface coated with Perfect Mount adhesive. Ideal for high-gloss photos. Repositionable until pressure is applied and then the adhesive makes a permanent bond.

PRESSURE-SENSITIVE FOAM BOARD (BIENFANG)
A smooth, clay-coated foam board featuring a pressure-sensitive adhesive coating on one side. Adhesive is aggressive for a permanent bond.

SELF ADHESIVE FOAMBOARD (NIELSEN BAINBRIDGE)
Smooth foam board coated with pressure-sensitive adhesive. High tack adhesive is initially repositionable. Available white or all black.

PRESSURE-SENSITIVE LAMINATING FILMS
BIENFANG makes a selection of pressure-sensitive laminating materials for use with roller style cold presses. Most are UV absorbent. Several finishes are available.

BASIC PRESSURE-SENSITIVE MOUNTING

1. Clean dust from artwork.

2. To begin, start at corner, use a fingernail to carefully lift the release paper to expose the adhesive. Take care not to separate the adhesive layer from the board.

Note: Do not touch the adhesive with hands, as oil from fingers will inhibit adhesion.

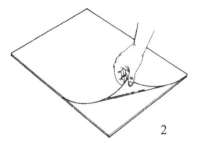

2

3. Pull back the release paper, exposing an edge of adhesive. Place the item on the exposed edge. Carefully pull the release paper from under the item, allowing the work to set on the adhesive surface.

4. Position and reposition the artwork until it is in the desired position. A board which is larger than the artwork may be used and trimmed after mounting.

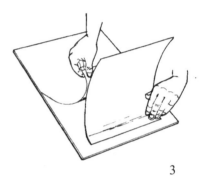

3

5. Check for air bubbles by holding the piece up to the light and inspecting the surface. Remove air bubbles by repositioning the piece.

6. Once the artwork is in the correct position, set therelease paper on the face of the item to avoid scratching the surface. Apply firm, even pressure with a plastic squeegee or burnisher. A mounting press may also be used (no heat necessary.)

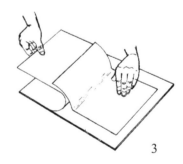

3

7. Store the finished piece flat for a minimum of 24 hours to allow the adhesive to cure.

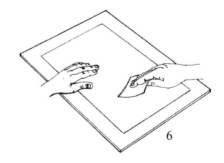

6

CHAPTER 5
SPRAY MOUNTING

Spray mounting is a quick way to bond two pieces of paper together. There are several types of spray adhesives, either chemical solvent-based or water-based.

The three basic elements to address with spray mounting are time (both open and bond time), pressure and moisture. Adequate time after applying the spray is required for the solvent to evaporate and the adhesive to become tacky. This is when the print may be aligned and repositioned if necessary, and is known as "open time." The ability of sprays to adhere is directly related to the type of adhesive and its *thorough* application. The initial bond is made within the first hour. If not using a press, pressure is required for 4-24 hours for the most permanent bond. The use of presses will hasten the bond.

Moisture in mounting boards, art and spray adhesives can affect the bond. Environmental moisture also has an impact—a suitable bond is more difficult to achieve in high humidity.

Most spray adhesives require good ventilation during use, and the excess sticky spray must be contained. A spray booth and/or ventilation hood to manage fumes and contain sprayed adhesive is highly recommended.

After spraying apply pressure using a press, or a brayer or burnisher can provide the pressure to create the bond. The sprayed item needs to be placed under a weight while drying or put in a press.

Spray mounting is not recommended for valued photographs. Spray mounting may be an inexpensive mounting alternative, but does not ensure long-term permanence. The permanence of spray mounting may increase with the use of a cold vacuum press. The vacuum press can provide strong, even pressure and remove any humidity present in the mounting package.

TIME
Time is required for the solvent in the spray to evaporate. The permanent bond of the two surfaces may require up to 24 hours.

TEMPERATURE
Warm temperatures will speed the bonding process.

MOISTURE
Moisture will disturb the best of spray adhesives. Keep art and boards dry.

PRESSURE
Bonding can be quick with the use of a press. Heat press: about 2 minutes, Cold press: about 5 to 15 minutes.

EQUIPMENT

All presses are suitable for use with sprays. Heat, cold, combination presses, and roller presses will provide the required pressure for spray glues. Presses are described on pages 24 and 25.

SPRAY BOOTH
A spray booth must be used with spray adhesives to gather the fumes and the glue solids which become airborne when aerosols are used.

BURNISHER
A burnisher, typically made of plastic, is used to apply pressure and for smoothing.

BRAYER
A brayer is used to apply pressure or to roll-on wet pastes. They are available in several sizes in soft or hard rubber or plastic.

KRAFT PAPER
Simple brown kraft paper, used in many frame shops as dust covers, can be used as a protective sheet in several mounting processes. It can be folded to make a protective envelope to hold the work, adhesive and substrate as it goes into the press. It can be used as a background layer for spray mounting to contain overspray. Kraft paper is smooth, absorbent and relatively inexpensive.

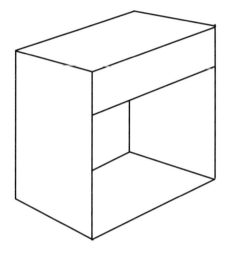

A small spray booth with a hood can be made from a sheet of foam center board. It will not protect from fumes but it will contain much of the spray.

SPRAY ADHESIVES

SUPER 77 (3M)

Translucent, high-tack, repositionable, non-staining, permanent aerosol adhesive. Resists humidity. Good aging properties. Use with paper, fabric, foils, foam center board, cardboard, wood, hardboard, plastics and felt.

PHOTO MOUNT (3M)

Permanent, clear, non-staining, repositionable bonding of photos including RC and Ilfochrome Classics. Excellent aging properties. Can be used to mount reproductions, graphic art presentations, maps, posters and signs.

VAC-U-MOUNT (3M)

Permanent, clear, non-staining, repositionable adhesive for use with cold vacuum presses. Good aging properties. Can be used for photos, lithographs, screen prints, maps, posters, certificates and fabrics. Clear and will not bleed through.

PRO-SPRAY SYSTEM® (3M)

Fast drying, permanent spray adhesive. Water-based for greater user safety (less fumes than solvent-based sprays and non-flammable). Two-part system includes cartridge of adhesive and pneumatic applicator with trigger pull.

EXTRA-STRENGTH SPRAY ADHESIVE (ELMER'S)

Sprays wide, dries fast and clear. Aggressive adhesive for a strong permanent bond.

"SPRAYABLE" PASTES

Some water-based adhesives such as SureMount® from PrintMount and Lamin-All® From McDonald Photo Products may be sprayed using a spray gun and compressor. It takes practice to get a fine, even layer of spray, but offers the benefits of a fine quality spray adhesive. The water content may be a problem, potentially causing buckling as the art paper absorbs moisture.

Basic Procedure for
Spray Mounting Paper Art

1. Cover work surface with kraft paper or newsprint to absorb test sprays and oversprays.

2. Lay the item to be mounted face down on the work surface. If the item is already trimmed, use a folded paper accordion to keep the edges up. This makes it easier to lift the sprayed piece when it is time to set it in position on the mounting board.

3. Shake the spray can well and do a test spray to make sure the can is working properly. Check the manufacturer's recommendations to determine the ideal spraying distance between the spray can nozzle and the item.

4. Begin to spray adhesive from the top and spray in rows to the bottom. Overspraying on the top, bottom and sides will insure that the adhesive covers the edges.

Note: Make sure to spray the adhesive evenly and thoroughly. Every inch of the item must be covered with adhesive.

5. Apply a second coat of adhesive, spraying rows of adhesive in the opposite direction of the first coat so that the rows crisscross.

6. Let the adhesive sit for 30 seconds, to allow the solvent to dissipate, so the adhesive gets tacky.

7. Position the print on the substrate.

8. Place on a hard surface such as glass or Masonite. Cover with kraft paper and smooth from the center to the edges using a flat hand or soft brayer.

9. Set flat under weight for extended time to allow the adhesive to dry and bond or place in a cold frame or a warm press.

10. Invert can and clear nozzle of remaining spray after use.

CHAPTER 6

PRICING MOUNTING SERVICES

PRICING MOUNTING SERVICES
by Robert Mayfield, CPF, GCF

Mounting, laminating and canvas transfer services should be priced to "stand on their own." Often these services are sold by themselves, not always as a part of a full framing job, so the price has to cover the cost of all materials used, the labor or time involved, the cost of the equipment, and a profit to keep the business operating and the employees paid.

Pricing is part of the four "P"s of marketing: *Place*, the location; *Product*, what is sold; *Promotion*, how the products are sold and *Price*, what the customer expects and what is profitable.

What segment of the retail marketplace do you want your shop to fit into? Do you want to serve the upper end segment that is not as price-sensitive or the lower, very price-sensitive marketplace, or somewhere in-between? Often theses decisions are made while developing the business plan and marketing strategy of the store.

Is your shop going to pursue mounting and laminating jobs in addition to those done in the normal course of framing? Competition for those jobs include: quick print shops, blue print shops, photo studios, memory-book stores, and graphic art and supply stores. This is another area that should be addressed in the business plan.

Mounting prices can be expressed in United Inches (UI) or square inches. Most frame shops use the United Inch method. United Inches is the sum of the width and the height of the art (8x10 =18 UI). The square inches or area of a job is figured by multiplying the height and the width (8x10=80 sq. inches.)

The basic formula for prices is:
Actual Material Cost multiplied by Markup, plus Labor, equals the Selling Price.

These basic components of the retail price include:

ACTUAL MATERIAL COST: This is the cost of the adhesive and other disposable supplies. Most shops charge for the board or substrate and the mounting service separately. This allows for the widely varying cost of the different substrates. The Actual Cost of the material is the invoiced cost of the supplies with Shipping, Waste and Carrying Charges added in. Shipping charges are the UPS or freight costs to deliver the supplies to your shop. If you pick up your supplies don't forget to factor in those costs. Waste or shrinkage is the material that ends up in the trash can or is ruined. Expressed as a percentage it can be as high as 25%. The carrying cost for your shop is the cost of capital or how much money is costing you. Expressed in another way: how much could you earn by investing in something other that your frame shop? How much are you paying on your credit card transactions?

MARKUP: This is the standard multiplier used in your shop to determine the selling price of items for resale in your shop. It is often 2 to 2.5 times.

LABOR COST: This is the cost of the labor necessary to perform the job. This includes the time needed to gather and prepare the supplies, the actual mounting, and the clean up. The time to wet mount an item is often greater than heat mounting, sharply reducing the advantage of the lower material cost. The time needed to perform the job is multiplied by the shop's labor rate not the employee's pay rate.

A quick way to calculate the shop labor rate is to look at the operating expenses listed on your 12-month financial statement. Divide this amount by the total direct labor hours for the same period. Direct labor is the labor attributed to production in the shop. If your operating expenses are $100,000 per year and your direct labor for the period totals 5,000 hours, then your labor cost would be $20.00 per hour. The labor cost has to be marked up just like any other commodity that you are selling. The usual markup is two times, so your shop labor rate in this example would be $40.00 per hour.

If you feature mounting and lamination services customers may ask for quantity discounts. Mounting is one service that can qualify for discounts if many of same items are being processed at the same time. There can be a significant savings in time (labor), therefore justifying quantity discount. The discounted price will still include a profit on the job. On a cost per item, the increased volume may slightly reduce the cost of materials per mounting piece, while labor should significantly be reduced. The discount is based on this direct labor savings.

Figure your costs of completing several different jobs using the formula:

Actual Material Cost multiplied by Markup, plus Labor, equals the Selling Price

To determine the retail charge per United Inch divide the cost by the united inches (UI) for that job to get the price per United Inch. To figure the charge per Square Inch divide the cost by the square footage of that job. Do this for several sizes and average the results to determine the retail selling price.

PRICING EXAMPLE FOR A 16X20 PIECE

For the example below, assume that:
- This shop uses a 2.25 markup
- The labor charge is $40/hour
- The mounting procedure will take 8 minutes to complete
- The tissue/freight/waste costs have already been calculated.

Also note that a 16x20 piece = 2.2 sq.ft.)([16x20] divided by 144.)

DETERMINE MATERIAL SELLING PRICE

Tissue per sq. ft.	+Freight	+Waste (20%)	=Actual Cost
$0.45/sq.ft.	$0.005/sq.ft.	$0.09/sq.ft	$.545/sq.ft.

Actual Material Cost	x Markup	=Material Selling Price
$0.545	2.25	$1.23/sq.ft.

Material Selling Price	x Quantity Used	=Material Price for this job
$1.23/sq.ft	2.22 sq.ft.	$2.73

Determine Retail Selling Price for Job

Hourly Rate	x Portion of Hour Used	= Labor
$40/hr	8/60 (8 minutes)	$5.33

Material Price	+ Labor	= Retail Price for this job
$2.73	$5.33	$8.06 + Plus retail price of substrate

To Determine the cost per United Inch

Retail Price	÷ United Inches (UI)	= Cost per United Inch
$8.06	(16 + 20 = 36)	$0.23

CHAPTER 7

PROJECTS

The following pages contain instructions for many of the most frequently requested mounting projects for custom framers. The methods suggested *seldom* address conservation. These instructions are intended to mount a piece for presentation. Sometimes a method may inadvertently preserve the piece from falling apart, but that is generally not the intention of the process.

Alternative methods of mounting are given along with instructions for the preferred method, since most frame shops will not have the equipment and materials to perform all mounting methods.

SOME GENERAL INFORMATION

The basic procedures for mounting methods appear on the following pages:
- Dry Mounting, page 30
- Wet Mounting, page 38
- Pressure-Sensitive Mounting, page 42
- Spray Mounting, page 46

GENERAL CAUTIONS WHEN MOUNTING ARTWORK:
- varnish on posters may crack
- plastic coatings may crack
- metallic (gold or silver) printing may shift in the heat press or adhere to release papers
- some thermoprinting processes discolor under heat and are sensitive to fingerprints
- sensitive giclées and ink jet prints

NEW PRINTING METHODS
Be very careful, because the number of items printed with heat-sensitive inks and/or papers is growing. These pieces may look like ordinary snapshots, even reproductions! These are very difficult to recognize; many are printed on very thin, slick, opaque paper. They are also sensitive to fingerprints. These items will have to be edge mounted or pressure-sensitive mounted.

EMBOSSED ART
During the mounting process, an embossed design on paper may flatten. When using heat methods putting a sponge pad over the face of the art reduces the risk of flattening. In the wet mount process, the embossing will soften and expand causing flattening of the design.

POSTERS AND REPRODUCTIONS

The term posters describes many different types of posters which may include:
- antique advertising posters
- original hand-pulled art show posters
- quality limited edition reproduction posters
- regular reproduction posters
- inexpensive copies of posters

Like all items for framing these may fall into the classification of investment pieces, sentimental items, historical documents or just decorative pieces.

Few problems arise with the decorative pieces, except a few of the new thermographic printing processes (see page 87.) The decision to permanently mount these is based on the importance to the customer and required end result.

Before proceeding with any mounting process, carefully wipe off the poster because posters and other printed graphics may have offset printing powder remaining; this must be removed before mounting, because the powders will resist adhesion.

ORIGINAL ART SHOW POSTERS
Prior to the 1980s many posters represented a specific art gallery exhibition and often were original screen prints or lithographed pieces. These should be mounted using conservation methods. See *Vol. 4, Conservation Framing.*

COLLECTOR ADVERTISING POSTERS
These posters may be actual antiques or current reproductions of the original posters. The antique originals were printed on a common wood pulp paper because they were intended for short term use as advertising. To retard the natural process of deterioration, the posters are often mounted to a fabric backing which also allows them to be rolled for shipping purposes. No, this is not conservation in the true sense, but it will help hold the deteriorating paper together. Although the fabric-back looks similar to the canvas backing on an oil painting, the poster must not be stretched over bars since the fabric will stretch but the paper poster will break apart under pressure.

- Use conservation hinges on fabric-backed or paper collector posters. Keep them away from the glass with mats or spacers.

- If an advertiser poster must be fabric-backed, use raw cotton duck (art supply store) with an archival dry mount tissue. Once mounted, it will probably not be removable, even if the adhesive manufacturer suggests that it will. The process of reheating and attempting to peel the poster off the backing will likely result in broken poster pieces.

- Wet mounting can be used. Choice of fabric weave is important for any mounting method used because if the weave is uneven and bumpy the texture will transfer to the image.

REPRODUCTIONS
The directions and cautions are virtually identical for both posters and reproductions. The product is nearly identical; paper, inks and printing processes. Value is the main concern when considering the permanent attachment of the poster or reproduction. Use conservation techniques if you suspect the piece to be of value.

Flush Mounting
a Poster or Reproduction
using a Heat-activated, Adhesive-
Coated Board

Flush mounting is a method that is used when the poster or reproduction will be trimmed to the edges. Often used when they are framed without a mat.

MATERIALS:
    Heat-activated, adhesive-coated board
    Tacking iron

1. Measure the poster and trim the sheet of adhesive board about 1" larger than needed. This will accommodate accidental shifting of the poster while it is being placed into the press. It is a lot easier to trim off excess than to try to add a piece of board.

2. Preheat dry mount press to appropriate temperature.

3. Pull the release paper off the board to expose the adhesive. Save the release paper; it can be used as a covering in the press. Do not let the release paper get dirty; the dirt will transfer to the poster. Both the adhesive board and the item to be mounted must be free of oil, wax, water and dirt particles.

4. Set the poster on the adhesive board. Use a tacking iron to tack one corner of the poster in place.

5. Cover the poster with the release paper and place in the press. Allow the item to remain in the press for the required dwell time. Remove from the press.

Note: If a thick cover sheet is used while the item is in the press, the cover will absorb much of the heat, reducing temperature by approximately 30°F.

6. Allow to cool while lying flat. A lite of glass may be set on top of the release paper to provide pressure.

7. Trim excess board away from print.

If the poster is larger than the dry mount press, use the multi-bite method on page 53.

3

5

6

LAMINATING A POSTER OR REPRODUCTION

These directions are for laminating a poster that has already been mounted to a backing board.

1. Wipe all dust and lint from the poster.

2. Use a piece of laminating film larger than the print, but smaller than the board. Perforate (pierce) the film if necessary. Pull back release paper exposing edge of film.

3. Set the edge of the film on the backing board just above the top of the poster.

4. Pull the release paper out from under the film allowing the film to lay on the poster. Use one hand to pull the release paper from under the film and another to smooth out any wrinkles in the film.

5. Assemble the mounting package as follows:

    > release paper
    > laminating film
    > poster mounted on backing board

6. Place it in the press using time and temperature determined by the mounting materials and the manufacturer's instructions for the laminating film.

7. Take out of press and trim as needed.

1

4

DRY MOUNT AND LAMINATE IN ONE STEP

To dry mount and laminate a poster or reproduction in one step, assemble the mounting package as follows:

> release paper
> laminating film (perforated)
> poster
> porous permanent adhesive
> substrate

OVERSIZED PRINTS

MOUNTING OVERSIZE PRINTS
IN A MECHANICAL HEAT PRESS

One of the advantages of a mechanical heat press is the ability to mount pieces that are larger than the press. Prints as wide as twice the depth of the press and of unlimited length can be mounted. This process requires making multiple successive bites with the press. The area around the press must be clear and free of obstructions. Large objects may require an additional person to provide support and help maneuver the piece.

1. Predry the board and print.

2. Use a permanent adhesive to prevent the releasing of the bond as it is reheated. Tack the piece where the first bite will be (in the center of one side.) Only tack in one place to prevent buckling of the adhesive and print.

3. Wearing a glove to protect the art, flatten print with a hand, forcing as much air from the package as possible. Check for dust.

Note: If using foam center board or some other soft mounting board, use a release board to prevent denting the mounting board. The release board should be larger than the platen. Remember to adjust the pressure for the increased thickness of the mounting package. The use of a release board will increase the dwell time needed for each bite. While it is tempting to increase the temperature of the press to speed up the process, it will make it more time-sensitive. Leaving the foam center board in too long may cause the board to compress from the high temperature, leaving lines on the project.

4. Take the first bite where the print has been tacked. If the print is wider than the depth of the press, the second bite will be on the opposite side. This will involve turning the whole package around. Do not mount one long side and then the other because this may lead to buckling or wrinkling. Alternate sides and work toward the ends of the board. If the print is smaller than the depth of the press, start in the middle and work toward each end.

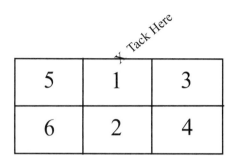

Mounting order for item that is wider and deeper than the press.

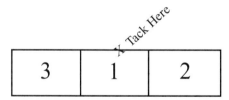

Mounting order for item that is smaller than the depth of the press.

SPECIAL CONSIDERATIONS WITH OVERSIZED ART ON PAPER

- What is the media? Follow directions for the specific type of media: paper poster, photograph, collectable poster calendar, etc. The adhesive should be chosen specifically for the media.

- Is there a substrate available in the size required? Both foam center board and rag matboard are available in 48x96".

PHOTOGRAPHS

The myriad of photography methods and materials makes it difficult to use the same process for every photo that must be mounted. Extensive and detailed information about framing photography and identifying the many types of photographs that are framed can be found in *Vol. 6, Framing Photography.*

MOUNTING OPTIONS FOR PHOTOGRAPHY:

- CONSERVATION EDGE STRIPS, mounting strips, pocket corners, sink mats. Detailed information can be found in *Volume 4, Conservation Framing.*

- DRY MOUNTING can be used for most photography. But great care must be taken with Ilfochrome Classics (Cibachrome) because the substrate and the finishing techniques make them very susceptible to scratching, even from the cover sheets meant to protect them. Test before applying heat whenever possible, as different photo printing processes have different heat tolerances.

- WET MOUNTING can be used for many types of photographs, but the choice of paste is important.

- PRESSURE-SENSITIVE MOUNTING is especially suitable for high gloss photographs The substrate is important because the texture of the backing board will transfer to the image.

- Most snapshots can be mounted with any process, except some of the new duplication processes are very heat- and fingerprint-sensitive.

POLAROID® PRINTS

These photos are both heat-sensitive and moisture-sensitive. It is best to use edge strips or corner mounts to support these photographs. If they must be fully mounted, use pressure-sensitive adhesives or spray adhesives.

Image Transfers
Four Polaroid prints have been transferred to an all cotton rag paper by the photographer. The image is now treated as art on paper and hinge mounted and matted, rather than fully mounted.

STATIC MOUNTING
OF POLYESTER-BASED PHOTOGRAPHS
AND OTHER FINE ART
by Paul MacFarland, CPF, GCF

Polyester-based photographs, such as Ilfochrome Classics® or computer generated fine art, present special problems in the mounting process. Because of their high gloss and ultra smooth surface, most conventional mounting methods may produce an "orange peel" effect, usually due to the lack of smoothness of the adhesive and/or the board. The "orange peel" effect is a series of small dents on the high gloss surface of a photograph.

Conventional preservation methods such as hinging with a water-based adhesive will not work, as the paste will not adhere to the plastic. Although pressure-sensitive tapes will stick, this method is at best temporary, because the pressure-sensitive adhesive will not penetrate the fiber of the plastic to complete a permanent bond, and will eventually fail.

Even if the plastic-based artwork is hinged, another problem arises. The center of the art or photo will most often bow outward toward the glazing, creating an irregular surface, distorting the image and often making contact with the glazing, a problem which is even worse when acrylic is used because the acrylic draws the photo towards its surface.

To avoid these problems, the static mounting method is employed. This method, especially helpful with large photos or artwork, uses a sheet of acrylic for the mounting surface instead of a paper mount board. The artwork is held in place by a combination of a static charge and photo corners or perimeter mounting flanges.

Static mounting will require a minimum of two people and a very clean work area. It is also important to use the utmost care in handling the artwork as any fingerprint, fine scratch, or wrinkle will permanently damage the work, and due to the high gloss and ultra smooth surface, will appear magnified when under glazing. Use white polyester gloves since cotton gloves produce lint. The surface of the artwork is so sensitive that anything that comes in contact with it will most often scratch it. This includes dust and most certainly the brush used to remove the dust. Therefore, try to prevent dust contact by keeping the artwork covered with interleaving tissue or the packaging it came in for as much of the process as possible. If the art is in a paper folder, remember that the shifting of the art in the folder can also damage the surface.

Suggestion: Do this kind of work early in the morning because there is less dust in the workroom.

MATERIALS:
  Sheet of acrylic
  T-square
  Pencil
  Utility Knife
  Photo

1. Cut a sheet of acrylic to the frame rabbet dimension, leaving the cover sheets on the acrylic.

2. Use a T-square and pencil to measure and mark the opening that will accommodate the photo. Add an extra 1/4 inch to the measurement for leeway.

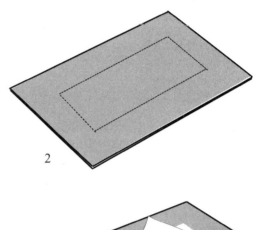

3. Cut along the marking with a sharp utility knife, making sure to cut through the paper cover; do not remove the cover sheet yet.

4. Prepare for mounting the artwork by having an assistant(s) hold the artwork by the edges, gently bowing the artwork into a "U" shape.

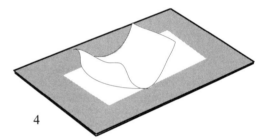

5. Peel up an edge of the cover sheet, just enough to firmly grasp it.

6. Quickly rip the cover sheet away to create as much static charge as possible and immediately place the artwork, center first, onto the acrylic sheet. A light downward pressure on the "U"-shaped artwork will allow the center to attach first, followed by the edges. *This can only be attempted once.*

7. The artwork should now be held in place by the static charge which will keep the center from bowing outward, but, to be safe, the edges should be attached with perimeter mounts, such as Lineco See-Thru Mounting Strips®, or Mylar/Melinex corner pockets.

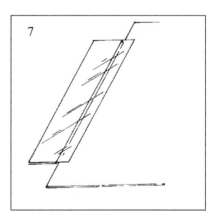

RC or resin coated photographs have a plastic base rather than paper, so mounting them can be tricky. Check the back for markings to identify the type of photograph.

Materials:
   Dry mount tissue
   Rag matboard
   Kraft paper
   Release Paper
   RC photo

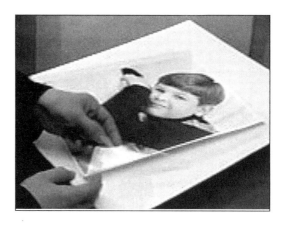

1. Cut a piece of rag matboard for the mount board.

2. Cut a piece of dry mount tissue.

3. Predry mount board, kraft paper and photograph.

4. Place the RC photograph face down on the predried kraft paper and cover the back of the photograph with tissue. Line up at least two edges of the tissue with two edges of the photograph.

5. Through a scrap of release paper, tack the tissue to the back of the photograph in one small spot on one edge. Trim to exact size of photo.

6. Position the photograph on the rag board. Lift the edge that is opposite of the previously tacked edge, lay down a piece of release paper and tack the tissue to the rag board through release paper.

7. Set the press to the temperature required by the adhesive and allow the unit to stabilize at that temperature.

8. Assemble the mounting package in the following order:
     Release Paper
     Photo
     Tissue
     Substrate
     Clean kraft paper

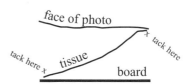

The "Z" tacking method: tack the tissue to the back of the photo and the top of the board.

9. Leave the mounting package in the press for 1-2 minutes. Time may vary with size and thickness of substrate.

10. Remove all materials as a unit from press and place them under a weight until cooled.

11. After the work has cooled, remove the cover sheet from the mounted photograph.

MOUNTING ILFOCHROME CLASSICS®
(CIBACHROME) USING SUPERSMOOTH®

These high-gloss photographs require a very smooth substrate. Any texture or imperfections in the mounting board will show.

MATERIALS:
> Smooth board precoated with Pressure-sensitive adhesive
> Brayer or roller
> Pair of polyester gloves for handling of the print

1. Trim a piece of board to appropriate size for the photograph. Don't touch the surface of the photograph. Finger prints may not be visible today but they may become visible over time, as a chemical reaction between the fingerprint oils and the chemicals used to make the photograph may occur.

2. Remove dust from photograph and mounting board.

3. To expose the adhesive on the board, start at the corner using a fingernail to carefully lift the release paper.

Although most items are repositionable, test a corner before setting the photograph in position. Special care should be taken with color photographs and glossy stock paper, as some stocks adhere more quickly than others to the adhesive.

4. Pull back the release paper, exposing several inches of the board. Place the photograph on the exposed edge. *Test first.* Pull the release paper from under the item, allowing the photograph to set on the adhesive surface.

5. Some photographs may be repositionable, however, Ilfochrome Classics seldom are. It is easier to select a board larger than needed and trim it to size after mounting.

6. Check for air bubbles by holding the piece up to the light and inspecting the surface. Remove air bubbles by lifting an edge and repositioning the photograph.

7. Once satisfied with the position, set the release paper on the face of the item to avoid scratching the surface. Gently smooth the print into position. Set under a lite of glass. A mounting press without heat may also be used to apply pressure.

8. Store finished piece flat, with a lite of glass as a weight, for 12 to 24 hours to allow the adhesive to cure.

MOUNTING A PHOTOGRAPH FOR A
PHOTOGRAPHIC COMPETITION

MATERIALS:
    Photo
    Pressure-sensitive adhesive film
    Art paper
    Competition Black matboard
    Ruler
    X-Acto Knife

1. Clean dust from the photograph, mounting board and art paper.

2. Apply pressure-sensitive adhesive film to the back of the photograph. Burnish film in place.

3. Apply pressure-sensitive adhesive film to the back of the art paper. Burnish in place.

4. Trim the photograph using a ruler and X-Acto knife. If the edges of the photo are dark, hold the knife at an angle when trimming to reduce visibility of the white photographic paper.

5. Trim the art paper 1" larger than the photograph.

6. Measure and mark the matboard for placement of the art paper. Accuracy counts.

7. Peel the release paper from the back of the art paper. Position the paper on the mount board. Burnish to secure.

8. Peel the release paper from the back of the photograph. Position the photograph on the art paper. Set the release paper on the face of the photograph, to avoid scratching the surface. Burnish to secure. Excessive pressure on the photograph may cause it to show an imprint of the texture of the art paper.

9. Store the finished piece flat, under a lite of glass, for 12 to 24 hours to allow the adhesive to cure. Do not bend or flex the board because this causes "tunneling" as the paper and adhesives are stretched.

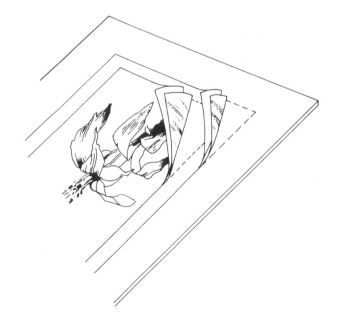

CANVAS TRANSFER

This method is used to transfer images to canvas, creating the look of a painting.

TRANSFERRING IMAGES TO CANVAS

This process can be accomplished using several methods of mounting, and can be done with photographs and reproductions.

The basic principle of canvas transfer begins with adhering a permanent laminating film to the face of the image, which attaches the printed image to the laminate. The backing paper is then stripped away leaving only the printed image on the laminating film. The stripped image is then mounted to a canvas. The fabric-mounted image can then be texturized to simulate a painting or other effect if desired.

Canvas for this purpose may be artist canvas sold in art supply stores or canvas with dry mounting adhesive already attached, which is available in the photo and framing industries.

After the transfer and canvas mounting process is complete, the transfer can be stretched on stretcher bars and framed.

Most commercially printed items on paper could be transferred to fabric: reproductions, posters, menus, greeting cards, photographs, etc. Using this process for personal use and as a request from a customer is probably all right in a legal sense, but be aware that issues of copyright arise whenever an original image is changed. Look into the copyright issue to be safe.

Canvas Transfers using Dry Mounting

Materials:
  Laminating film
  Dry mount adhesive
  Soft scrubber
  Print on paper
  Bucket of water
  Canvas precoated with adhesive
      (or piece of dry mount tissue and canvas fabric)

1. Remove release paper from laminate film. Place the print face up on the release paper. Lay the film on top of the print.

2. Place in press for the dwell time required for the laminate.

3. Remove laminated print from press and soak in a tub of water for 10-15 minutes depending on the thickness of the paper. The print may also be sprayed with water until it is thoroughly wet. Some papers require little wetting, but only testing will tell.

4. After thoroughly wet, lay the print face down on a clean surface. Peel the back of the paper off of the print leaving only the ink which has bonded to the laminate. A kitchen cleaning pad may help completely remove the paper backing. Dip print into water again to clean off small particles. Then place print on paper towel to dry.

5. Cut a piece of dry mount adhesive-coated canvas (or uncoated canvas plus tissue) 2" bigger on all sides than the print, to provide enough fabric to stretch the mounted print over stretcher bars. If the final image is to be mounted onto a board, then no extra canvas is necessary.

6. Pull back the release paper, exposing several inches of the adhesive-coated canvas. Place the laminated image on the exposed edge. Pull the release paper from under the item, allowing the image to set on the adhesive surface. If uncoated canvas is being used, then place the dry mount adhesive on the canvas and the laminated image on the adhesive.

7. Place a sheet of sponge foam on top of print. Put the mounting package back in the press for the dwell time required for the adhesive. The transferred image is now ready to be mounted on stretcher bars or board.

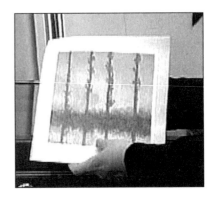

7

CANVAS TRANSFERS
USING PRESSURE-SENSITIVE METHODS

Canvas transfers can be done with pressure-sensitive materials made especially for this purpose. Finishes include matte and glossy, plus textures such as linen, sand, and leather embossed.

Pressure-sensitive adhesives may then be used to attach the print to the canvas, but a lot of pressure is required to force the print and the film into the weave of the fabric. Try using a hair dryer to warm the adhesive to encourage it to melt into the fabric. Then use a brayer to force the film into the weave. Put a sponge pad or release paper on top of the print, then a lite of glass and additional weight (such as books, or cans of paint) and allow the adhesive to become permanent.

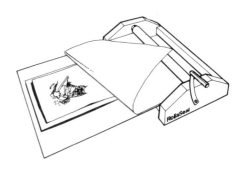

CANVAS TRANSFERS USING WET MOUNTING

Canvas transfers can be done with minimal equipment using wet pastes.

MATERIALS:
Polymer Medium
Canvas
Release Paper
Weight or Press
Tray or pan of water

1. Use a white polymer (such as Mod Podge, Liquitex polymer medium or Liquitex Soluvar) to coat the surface of the print to be transferred. Use a gloss or semi-gloss finish, as the matte finishes contain white pigment that will give the finished product a milky appearance.

2. Once the coating has dried thoroughly, soak the print in water for 15 minutes. Remove from water, lay face down on flat surface. Peel off the back, leaving the image attached to the polymer layer. Rinse off the bits and pieces and pat dry.

3. Brush polymer medium on a piece of canvas or woven fabric that is larger than the print.

4. Set the transferred print onto the pasted canvas or woven fabric.

5. Press print with a soft cloth to force the print into the weave of the fabric.

6. Set a piece of release paper on the surface of the print, then a weight to keep the print flat until it dries. A cold vacuum press hastens the drying process. If using a press, place a sponge pad on the surface of the transferred print. No weights are needed with the press.

When dry, the canvas is ready to be mounted to stretcher bars and framed.

Canvas and other fabrics must be stretched before framing. There are several stretching methods, but the following technique using stretcher bars and staples is the time honored tradition for paintings on canvas, and is often used with needlepoint and decorator fabrics as well.

MATERIALS:

Staple gun and staples (or hammer and tacks)
Canvas pliers
Measuring tape and pencil

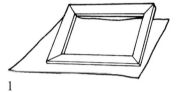

1. Select (or make) the stretcher bars—two for the length, two for the width. Fitted together, the four bars form a frame on which to stretch the canvas or material.

   There should be about 1-1/2" of canvas on each side for stretching. For example, a canvas to be stretched on 16x20" stretchers needs to be about 19x23". An experienced framer can stretch a canvas with just 1/2" of excess fabric on each side, but it is much easier if there is an inch or more to work with.

2. Square the stretcher frame by lining it up against a carpenter's square.

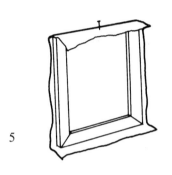

3. Measure to find the middle of each side of the canvas and the stretcher bars and mark with a pencil. This is very important to the successful stretching process.

4. Match up pencil marks on the short sides of the canvas and stretcher bars.

5. Fold the material margin over one of the short sides of the frame and fasten in the center with a staple gun.

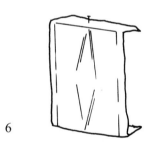

6. Reverse to the opposite side. Using canvas pliers to hold the edge of the canvas, stretch until canvas is taut; staple in the center, matching pencil marks.

7. Turn the frame so one of the longer sides is up. Grip and pull until diagonal wrinkles can be seen from the first two staples to the point where it is stretching, then staple in the center.

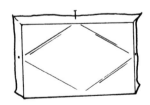

8. Repeat on the fourth side, pulling material until a diamond shaped set of four wrinkles has formed, and staple at the center.

9. Move pliers a couple inches to the left of center staple and staple again. Repeat in the same direction, stapling every two inches, working to the corner of the frame. Now do the same from the center to the right, but stop about 3" from the corner.

10. Do the same on the opposite long side leaving 3" at the right end unfastened. Repeat the process on the other two sides.

11. Finish the corners last, folding the material under itself and pulling it snug. Staple securely.

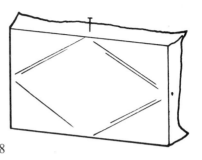

8

TIPS FOR WORKING WITH STRETCHER BARS

Manufactured stretcher bars often come with triangular wooden or plastic "corner keys." They are designed to fit into the slots in each corner of the stretcher after the canvas has been stretched; this creates a tighter stretch, which can be tightened even more in the future by tapping the keys further into the slots. There is much debate about the use of keys. Some believe they offer an effective way to maintain a taut canvas, but others have observed that the keys disfigure the canvas over time by pushing out the corners.

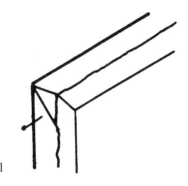

11

Do not trim off excess canvas. It is considered a part of the painting, just as the excess paper around a fine art print is considered a part of the art. Just fold excess canvas neatly on the back of the stretcher bars and tack with staples.

For conservation framing of canvas and fabric, seal the wooden stretcher bars with two or three coats of acrylic polymer medium, or cover them with aluminum barrier tape such as Lineco's Frame Sealing Tape. Be sure to use stainless steel staples in the staple gun.

FABRIC BACKING
FOR MAPS & CHARTS

Some companies make an adhesive-coated linen fabric specifically designed to reinforce or strengthen heavily used items such as field maps, blueprints and charts. The adhesive is generally heat-activated.

MATERIALS:
> Map
> Release paper
> Adhesive-backed fabric
> Tacking iron
> Scrap board larger than map

1. Predry the map.

2. Cut fabric backing to required size. Tack map to adhesive-backed fabric.

3. Assemble the mounting package (top to bottom):
   > top release paper
   > map
   > adhesive-backed fabric
   > bottom release paper
   > matboard for support

4. Place in press and mount at the suggested temperature and time for the adhesive.

5. Remove entire package from press. Cool under weight.

Once the map has cooled, it can be rolled or folded.

You can make your own fabric adhesive-coated fabric using raw cotton and a soft film adhesive.

FABRICS

Most fabric can be mounted to matboard or foam center board. Dry mounting, wet mounting, pressure-sensitive, and even spray mounting can be used to mount fabrics. Fabric mounted to a board can be used for covered mats or as a backing board for a shadow box. See page 70 for the Quick Box technique.

VERY THIN fabrics (silks, sheers, and gingham) require adhesives that will not bleed into the fibers. The backing board and the adhesive should be chosen carefully because they will show through the fabric. As long as these requirements are met, all mounting methods can be used.

MEDIUM thickness fabrics, such as khaki, cotton, and linen can be mounted with any method.

THICK fabrics such as velvets, velveteen, brocades, tapestry, and wool may require thick adhesive (a wet paste or multiple layers of a dry mount film) that will bond securely to the fibers.

CREATING A FABRIC-COVERED MAT USING A HEAT PRESS

MATERIALS:
    Mat with window opening (for ovals, the opening
        fallout is needed)
    Release paper
    Heat-activated tissue
    X-Acto knife or razor blade
    Fabric
    Tacking iron

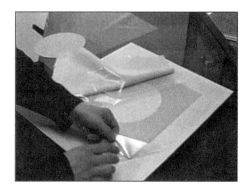

1. Align dry mount tissue with edges of mat. Tack tissue to face of mat. Tack only in one spot.

2. Tack the fabric to the tissue, again tacking only in one spot.

3. Note: If covering an oval, place the oval fallout on top of the fabric before covering with release paper. Place a sheet of release paper on the top and bottom of the mounting package.

4. Put the mounting package into press. Dwell time depends on the type of adhesive tissue and thickness of the fabric.

3

5. Remove from the press. If fabric is thick or stubborn, place it under a lite of glass or weights while it cools.

6. Trim off any excess fabric from the outside of the mat.

7. Place mat face down and slice the fabric in the window opening; cut almost all the way to the corners.

   Note: When working with an oval, remove the center portion of the fabric, leaving enough to wrap around the mat opening. Then cut the fabric in many places around the opening to allow for a smooth wrap.

8. Fold over the flaps and tack to the back of the mat. Place in the press to bond. Use the tacking iron to finish edges if necessary.

CREATING A FABRIC-COVERED MAT USING PRESSURE-SENSITIVE MOUNTING

MATERIALS:
    Sheet of pressure-sensitive adhesive
    Squeegee or cold mount press
    Mat with opening (cut with a reverse bevel)
    Fabric

1. Apply adhesive to back of fabric. Squeegee to bond.

2. Peel cover sheet from adhesive and apply fabric to the face of the mat. Line up fabric weave.

3. Squeegee to bond.

4. Place fabric-covered mat face down to cut out window of fabric—careful of the corners.

5. Wrap fabric over bevel and secure.

6. Use squeegee or cold mount press to create the overall bond.

6

7

8

WET MOUNTING A FABRIC-COVERED MAT

MATERIALS:
    Mat with opening (cut with reverse bevel)
    Wet Mounting paste
    Brush
    Fabric

1. Apply mounting paste to the front of the mat.

2. Lay the fabric on the wet paste. Be sure the woven lines are parallel to the edges of the mat. There is no excuse for wavy lines or a weave that dives into the rabbet of the frame.

3. Turn the mat—fabric side down—and cut the fabric out of the window. Careful of the corners.

4. Apply the wet mounting paste to the sliced area. Wrap the four sections to the underside of the mat. Watch for excess paste in the corners—wipe it up right away.

5. If a vacuum press is available—it will apply needed pressure as well as take out the moisture. If not, put the piece under a lite of glass or other weight and allow to dry.

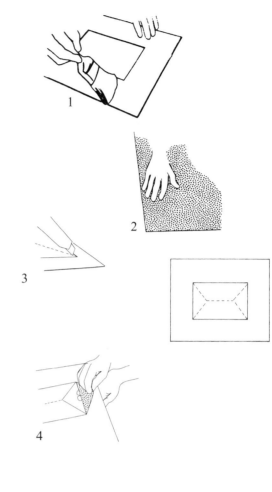

SPRAY MOUNTING A FABRIC-COVERED MAT

MATERIALS:
    Spray adhesive
    Squeegee, roller or vacuum press
    Mat with opening and reverse bevel
    Fabric

1. Spray both the face of the board and back of fabric in both directions. It is very important to get a full coverage of adhesive on both surfaces for a good bond to develop.

2. Set fabric on board. Line up grain of fabric with edge of board.

3. To bond, use a vacuum press or place a sheet of clean paper on the face of fabric and apply pressure with squeegee or roller.

4. Cut fabric in mat opening, turn flaps to back and attach to back of mat.

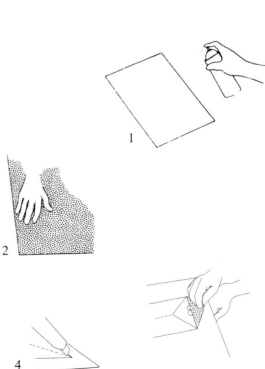

The Quick Shadow Box can be used to support light-weight items in a shadow box; it is perhaps the easiest method to create sides and a background at the same time. This type of box is especially fast when made with fabric-covered boards.

To make a Quick Box, a board is cut and folded. Measuring for the box must be done carefully—in order for the unit to fit in the frame, it is important to allow for the thickness of the board when it is folded to create the sides of the box.

MATERIALS:
    Fabric
    Mounting adhesive
    Mounting board
    Ruler
    Blade for scoring board
    Pressure-sensitive tape

1. Mount the fabric to the board. Fabric can be mounted using any of the methods: dry, wet, spray or pressure-sensitive.

2. Place the board face down and score (cut partially through) the back of the board where the fold should be.

3. Cut out and remove the four square corner pieces.

4. Fold the ends up and tape the corners on the outside with pressure-sensitive tape such as 3M#810 or linen tape.

ALTERNATE QUICK BOX METHOD
This method creates very neat interior corners with no seams in the fabric.

1. Place the board face down and score the back of the board where the fold should be.Cut out and remove the four square corner pieces.

2. Mount fabric to the board. Use a larger piece of fabric than needed, then trim after mounting—but leave the fabric in the corners.

3. Fold the sides of the box upwards. Neatly fold the protruding fabric at each corner. Tape the corners securely with pressure-sensitive tape such as 3M#810 or linen tape.

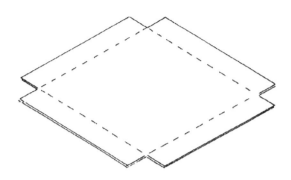

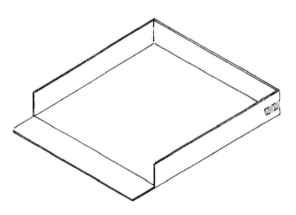

Note: If the item to be placed in the box is heavy, then a strong, dense board such as heavy duty foam board will be necessary as the substrate for the fabric. Check the rabbet depth of the frame moulding to make sure it can accommodate the thickness of the foam board and the depth of the box.

Newsprint and Other Thin Papers

Mounting Newsprint
using Pressure-Sensitive Film

Newspaper and magazine clippings may have printing on the reverse side that may be visible when the item is mounted. To minimize this, mount them on a dark, smooth matboard (such as black, dark brown or gray.) Apply mounting film to the newspaper first, trim excess adhesive, then mount to a board.

Do not use wet methods on newsprint, including magazines. Use pressure-sensitive adhesives, dry mounting, or sprays.

Materials:
    Dark backing board
    Pressure-sensitive film
    Burnisher or brayer

2

1. Set the film on a flat surface. Pull back the release paper exposing an edge of adhesive.

2. Place the clipping on the exposed adhesive. Carefully pull the release paper from under the item, allowing the artwork to set on the adhesive film. The film may wrinkle if the release paper is pulled off too quickly. Newspaper is soft and may tear easily—be careful to set the clipping down evenly. If clipping is small, place very carefully.

Note: If a full sheet of newspaper is being mounted, roll it onto a tube then unroll slowly while mounting, to control the placement on the adhesive.

4

3. Once the clipping is properly positioned—set the release paper on the face and smooth lightly. Do not push too hard—excessive pressure may force the clipping to stretch, slip or wrinkle.

4. Using a ruler and a blade, trim off excess film. A grid-marked cutting surface works nicely. Precise measurements and straight lines are very important when trimming the clipping.

5. Measure and mark the matboard for placement of the clipping.

6. Carefully peel back the release paper from the underside of the artwork exposing an edge of adhesive.

7. Set this edge in position on the matboard. Slowly pull the release paper from under the clipping while smoothing out wrinkles and bubbles. If the clipping is small, place a piece of release paper under the upper portion of clipping while positioning on matboard.

8. Once the artwork is positioned, set the release paper on the face of the item to avoid scratching the surface. Apply firm, even pressure with a plastic squeegee. A mounting press may also be used; no heat is necessary.

9. Store finished piece flat for 8 to 24 hours to allow the adhesive to cure. A lite of glass on top of the release paper may be used to provide pressure.

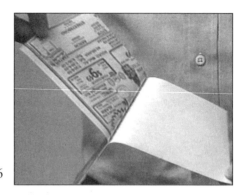

6

7

SPECIAL CONSIDERATIONS WITH NEWSPRINT

Newsprint pages or articles are thin papers that need support. The printing on the back of the page will show through the front if the piece if not handled correctly.

When mounting newsprint, use a dark gray or black matboard as the backing. The dark gray will minimize show-through.

Newsprint can be mounted with dry mount methods or pressure-sensitive adhesives.

Before mounting, newsprint can be deacidified to neutralize the lignin and chemicals that help newsprint degrade for recycling purposes. Instructions for using deacidification sprays are covered in *Volume 4, Conservation Framing*. Newsprint will discolor; it will return to color of tree pulp (tan.) As it darkens, it disintegrates. Mounting will hold the fibers together.

MAGAZINE PAGES
Flimsy and slick, magazine pages are essentially coated newsprint. Mount them in the same manner as newsprint. Glossy papers do not usually benefit from deacidification.

Dry Mounting Newsprint

MATERIALS:
Mounting tissue
Release paper
Substrate
Newspaper clipping

THIS IS A TWO STEP MOUNTING PROCESS

1. Set the newspaper onto a piece of dry mount tissue.

2. Use a tacking iron to hold the two together. Place the two pieces into a folded envelope of release paper. This will protect both sides of the unit.

3. Place in heated press to adhere the tissue to the newspaper.

4. Remove from press and peel the mounted unit from the release paper.

5. Use a ruler and X-Acto knife to trim the news article to size.

SECOND STEP:

6. Tack the unit in place on the board.

7. Cover with release paper and return to press.

8. Remove from press and proceed with framing.

2

5

7

BRASS RUBBINGS

MOUNTING A BRASS RUBBING
USING PRESSURE-SENSITIVE ADHESIVE

Brass rubbings are often done on soft, absorbent papers such as thin, black kraft paper or various Japanese papers. They pose a problem because the image is made by rubbing a wax-type crayon or paste on the face of the soft, thin paper. The rubbing framed on this page is done on rice paper, also called Japanese paper or Oriental paper.

Both the media and the papers are heat- and moisture-sensitive. Heat may melt the wax media, while wet pastes may seep through the thin paper.

MATERIALS:
    Pressure-sensitive film
    Sturdy mounting board (extra strength foam board)
       or a board with adhesive film already mounted
    Mailing tube
    Squeegee
    Weight

1. Apply the adhesive to the mounting board. Use a strong foam board which is rigid and will not flex; this is very important when working with stretchy paper.

2. Roll the rubbing onto a mailing tube to allow better control when setting the art onto the adhesive.

3. Pull back the release paper exposing an edge of adhesive.

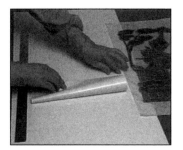

3

4. Place the top edge of the rubbing on the exposed adhesive. Carefully pull the release paper from under the rubbing while allowing the rubbing to set onto the adhesive. Continue to expose the adhesive and lay down the rubbing while smoothing out wrinkles and bubbles. Work slowly—the rubbing may wrinkle if this process is done too fast.

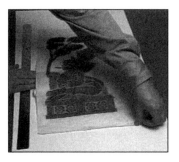

5

5. Lift slowly and carefully if need to reposition.

6. Once correctly positioned, set the release paper on the face of the artwork and smooth lightly. Apply firm, even pressure with a plastic squeegee. Do not push too hard because excessive pressure may force the rubbing to stretch, slip or wrinkle.

A mounting press may also be used to apply pressure; do not use heat.

7. Store finished piece flat for 8 to 24 hours to allow the adhesive to cure. A lite of glass on top of the release paper will provide even pressure during curing.

Even after curing is complete, be careful not to bend or flex the board because it will stretch the paper and the adhesive which can cause "tunneling."

6

MOUNTING TO THE CENTER OF A BOARD

If the rubbing is on light color paper, be sure to check for show-through before mounting on a color surface board.

To float the artwork in the center of a color surface board:

1. Cut a piece of board larger than actually needed.

2. Apply pressure-sensitive film to the back of the rubbing

3. Mount the adhesive-backed rubbing to the mount board.

4. Trim the board to the required size.

ALTERNATIVE MOUNTING METHODS FOR RUBBINGS:

- Some rubbings on heavier paper may be carefully wet mounted.

- Some of the wax crayons used for rubbings can withstand some heat. Always test carefully for heat sensitivity before attempting any heat method on a rubbing. If the test shows heat tolerance, then dry mount using the lowest temperature and shortest dwell time possible.

Wet Mounting A Rubbing

The rubbing framed here was done on thin, black paper. For these rubbings, mounting to a black or other dark color board helps maintain the color intensity of the rubbing.

MATERIALS:
  Paste
  Weight (glass or metal)
  Sturdy substrate
  Spray mister for water
  Scrap of glass & roller or brayer for pastes
  Brush and bowl for thin glues

1. Pour the paste on the glass, then roll the brayer back and forth to make an even layer of adhesive. A brush works better for thin glues. Do not use a piece of matboard to hold the paste—it will absorb the water in the paste and make the paste dry too fast.

2. Mist the back of the rubbing to expand the fibers of the paper. It will wrinkle—don't panic, it will flatten out on the wet-pasted mount board.

3. Apply the paste to the mount board. The application should be as even as possible. If it is too thick the print will dent on the surface—too thin and it will dry before the print is set in place. The entire surface must be covered with the paste.

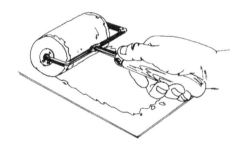

4. Carefully position the damp print onto the pasted area of the mount board. Use a cover sheet to protect the face of the print—remember, it is a wax media. Smooth the print in place using a brayer or soft brush. (A hand is not as smooth as a brayer and may leave finger indentations.

5. Set the rubbing under a lite of glass to dry or put into a vacuum press.

PRACTICE HELPS
This is an easy method to practice because the paper typically used for wax rubbings is similar to, if not exactly, brown kraft paper (20 lbs).

PRE-LAMINATED ITEMS

MOUNTING CALENDARS, PLACEMATS & MENUS USING PRESSURE-SENSITIVE BOARD

Items which are already laminated pose a problem because mounting films do not stay attached to the laminate. Wet pastes are not suitable and sprays will not hold for a long period of time. That leaves pressure-sensitive adhesive, which works very well because a polyvinyl acrylic adhesive will hold onto the laminated surfaces.

MATERIALS:
   Board coated with pressure-sensitive film
   Squeegee or burnisher
   Weight

1. Clean dust from item. Wipe with alcohol. Be sure to remove adhesive labels and tags.

2. Trim board to size. Starting at a corner, use a fingernail to carefully lift the release paper to expose the adhesive. Take care not to separate the adhesive layer from the board.

Note: Do not touch the adhesive with hand, as oil from fingers will inhibit adhesion.

3. Pull back the release paper, exposing an edge of adhesive. Place the laminated item on the exposed edge. Carefully pull the release paper from under the item, allowing the work to set on the adhesive surface.

4. Position and reposition the item until it is in the desired position. For easier positioning, a board which is larger than the artwork may be used and trimmed after mounting.

5. Check for air bubbles by holding the piece up to the light and inspecting the surface. Remove air bubbles by repositioning the piece and smoothing.

6. Once the artwork is in the correct position, set the release paper on the face of the item to avoid scratching the surface. Apply firm, even pressure with a plastic squeegee or burnisher. A mounting press may also be used (no heat.)

7. Store the finished piece flat for a minimum of 24 hours to allow the adhesive to cure.

PUZZLES

MOUNTING A PUZZLE
USING PRESSURE-SENSITIVE BOARD

MATERIALS:
    Board with pressure-sensitive adhesive
    Ruler and Pencil
    X-Acto Knife
    Burnisher
    Weight
    Puzzle

1. Measure the puzzle and the desired mat borders to arrive at the frame size. Cut a piece of pressure-sensitive board to the frame size.

2. Slide the puzzle onto a scrap of matboard approximately 1" larger than the puzzle.

3. Measure from the edge of the pressure-sensitive board to find the puzzle placement. Lightly draw the rectangle directly on the release paper with a pencil.

4. Using an X-Acto knife, carefully cut along the pencil lines through the release paper only—do not cut into the board or adhesive.

5. Lift the release paper from the center area exposing the adhesive.

6. Slide the puzzle from the scrap matboard onto the adhesive by setting one edge of the puzzle on the adhesive and slowly allowing the rest of the puzzle to drop onto the adhesive.

7. Check the puzzle for exact fit and positioning of pieces.

8. Set the release paper on the face of the puzzle as a cover sheet. Burnish the puzzle. Leave the release paper on the face of the puzzle. Set a lite of glass on top to provide pressure, then let the puzzle set for 12 to 24 hours to allow the adhesive to firmly bond.

Note: If there are no pre-coated pressure-sensitive boards on hand, a pressure-sensitive board may be created by applying double-sided pressure-sensitive film to a mounting board.

A NOTE ABOUT COLLECTIBLE PUZZLES:
Some are limited edition puzzles, and these should not be fully mounted. Following conservation standards, place limited edition puzzles in a sink mat, covered with a layer of polyester film (Mylar/Melinex) that is attached to the edges of the sink mat surface. Then add matting and glass.

WET MOUNTING A PUZZLE

MATERIALS:
   Paste
   Mount board
   Roller or brayer
   Weight
   Puzzle
   Release paper

1. Cut substrate to size predetermined for framed puzzle. Mark placement of puzzle on substrate.

2. Apply paste in an even coat, completely covering area on substrate where puzzle will be placed.

3. Place the puzzle on a scrap of matboard approximately 1" larger than the puzzle.

4. Slide the puzzle from the scrap matboard onto the adhesive. Set one edge of the puzzle on the adhesive and slowly allow the puzzle to drop onto the wet adhesive layer.

5. Smooth puzzle onto adhesive. Place in a vacuum press, cold dry mount press, or under a weight until adhesive is firmly set.

HEAT MOUNTING A PUZZLE
A puzzle may also be dry mounted using mounting film.

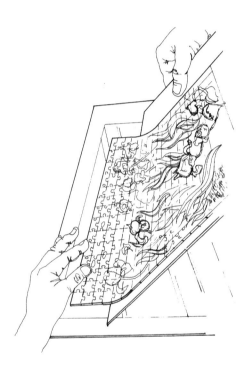

COLLAGES

MOUNTING A COLLAGE OF CARDS
EDGE-TO-EDGE USING PRESSURE-SENSITIVE BOARD

Valued sports or other collectible cards require conservation methods, but decorative cards may be fully mounted.

Materials:
Pressure-sensitive board
Ruler and Pencil
Mat cutter or X-Acto Knife
Burnisher
Cards

1. Arrange the cards, with the edges touching, in the desired design, prior to mounting. Measure the outside dimensions.

2. Add the size of the mat to the size of the card arrangement and cut the pressure-sensitive board to the resulting size.

3. Measuring inward from the edge of the pressure-sensitive board, draw the outline of the card arrangement directly on the release paper with a pencil.

4. Carefully cut along the pencil lines, cutting the release paper only—do not cut into the board or adhesive. If the arrangement covers a large area, cut the release paper in several sections to reveal smaller areas at one time.

5. Lift a section of the release paper from the board exposing the adhesive.

6. Position and reposition the cards on the adhesive. Continue exposing sections of adhesive and positioning cards until the desired placement has been achieved.

7. Set the release paper on the cards and burnish.

8. Set a lite of glass on the release paper for 12-24 hours to allow the adhesive to create a secure bond.

9. Remove all of the release paper and set the mat in place.

A set of 100 Marilyn Monroe cards.

6

COLLAGE OF SNAPSHOTS USING PRESSURE-SENSITIVE BOARD

MATERIALS:
Snapshots
Pressure-sensitive board
Burnisher or brayer

1. Plan the layout of the snapshots. Add for the size of the mat border. Trim the pressure-sensitive board to size.

Many snapshots have "extra" areas that are not the actual feature of the photo. These areas can be "trimmed" by covering them with a mat.

2. Pull release paper completely off of the pressure-sensitive board.

3. Lay snapshots edge-to-edge to duplicate layout previously designed. Use a small T-square to line up the photos.

4. Once the photographs are in the exact position, place release paper on snapshots and burnish with a squeegee or brayer.

5. Set a lite of glass on the release paper for 12-24 hours to allow the adhesive to create a secure bond.

6. The mat may then be placed over the mounted snapshots, directly on the pressure-sensitive board. All extra edges can then be trimmed.

1

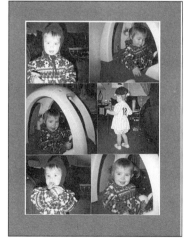

2

3

6

Mounting a Collage
of Floating Photographs
by Allan R. Lamb, CPF

1. Mount photographs to a non-buffered 100% cotton matboard (rag mat.)

Note: If the photographs to be mounted are the only copies or have faded, it is best to copy the originals and frame the copies.

2. Cut the photographs out of the backing board. A bevel cut will create a line of white, black or color depending on the core of the board being used. Or a reverse bevel may be used and no core will show.

3. Cut an oval out of the back ma t for the large photograph. Use a piece of non-buffered rag mat to separate the window mat from the photograph. See illustration below.

4. Place spacer mats under all the smaller photographs so that they float above the back mat. Some photographs should have more spacer mats beneath them to allow overlap. In this example, the rectangular photographs overlap.

Note: The photographs must not touch the glass.

The spacers should be 3/8" to 1/2" smaller than the photograph. If the spacers are too small, the photograph may warp. If too large, they will show. All spacers should be made out of matboard.

Note: Many types of photographs, including those shown in this projects, are sensitive to excessive alkalinity. Only non-buffered rag matboard should be used in contact with such photographs.

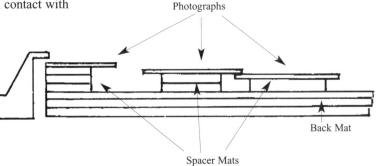

Photographs

Spacer Mats

Back Mat

VOLUME MOUNTING

PRODUCTION DRY MOUNTING
by William Parker, CPF, GCF

When deciding how to price quantity dry mounting jobs, first determine the cost of materials, including substrates, mounting tissue, and release paper. Then consider the space requirements for doing the job and storing the finished pieces. Then comes the tricky part—determining how much time the job will take.

Here are the pre-production steps for dry mounting posters, with the optimum time estimate and the actual time recorded in the frame shop.

BEST CASE	ACTUAL	
10 sec.	30 sec.	Place foam board on surface
30 sec.	30 sec.	Measure poster for tissue needs
20 sec.	30 sec.	Measure and tear tissue
10 sec.	20 sec.	Place tissue and poster on board
20 sec.	30 sec.	Secure with tacking iron
20 sec.	20 sec.	Trim excess tissue

To maximize efficiency and reduce time needed, be creative and consider ways the shop can be adapted to streamline the process.
For example:
- Work after hours, or set aside time when no other work will be done in the shop
- Work "production-style"; Measure all of the posters, then cut tissue for all of the posters, then tack all of the posters, etc.
- Temporarily rearrange the shop for easier production.

A vacuum press can accommodate several pieces at one time, making volume mounting efficient.

PRODUCTION WET MOUNTING
by Bob Mayfield, CPF, GCF
This method works well for a large quantity of small reproductions.

- Prepare all mount boards in advance.
- Set a sheet of glass larger than the largest print next to the press.
- Spread the paste onto the glass sheet to a uniform thickness with a roller.
- Place the print in the center of the paste.
- Use a palette knife to pick up the print at the corner.
- Set the print onto the mount board and smooth down.
- Place board and print in a vacuum press or under weight until adhesive is set. If excessive paste squeezes from under the print, apply a thinner coat to the glass next time.
- The process is then repeated for the next print. A spray bottle of water can be used to spray the glass and adhesive to maintain proper consistency.

REINFORCING ARTWORK

REINFORCING BROKEN, BRITTLE PAPER

Often someone wants to keep a piece of paper that is damaged or so brittle and weak that it cannot safely be framed. While items of significant value should be sent to a paper conservator for repair and restoration, many items may not warrant the expense.

With the consent of the owner of the broken or brittle paper item, pre-adhesived mending tissues made specifically for this purpose can be used as a support. Some are heat-activated, others have a wettable, water-based adhesive. Both types are considered permanent because any attempt to remove these will result in destruction of the piece. The tissues are sheer, which allows the mounted item to be seen on both sides.

To repair a small tear on a document using heat-activated tissue, tear (do not cut) a piece of the tissue a little larger than the tear to be repaired. Position the adhesive face down on the back of the artwork, making sure the overlapping edges of the tear are aligned correctly. A tacking iron (set at about 200 degrees F) is used to activate the adhesive. On larger pieces a heat press may be used.

HEAT-ACTIVATED TISSUE ENCAPSULATION
Paper can be fully encased in tissue as a reinforcement. Cut two pieces of tissue larger than the paper that will be mounted. In humid areas the paper should be pre-dried, but let it cool to prevent the tissue from sticking prematurely or curling up from the heat. Place the paper between the two sheets of tissue with the adhesive sides facing toward the paper. Flatten the package forcing out any excess air. Place in a heated press with a cover sheet of release paper. The press temperature will be determined by the adhesive manufacturer.

WATER-BASED ADHESIVE TISSUE MOUNTING
This tissue offers a method for mending and reinforcing papers that should not be subjected to heat. It is Japanese mulberry tissue with wheat starch paste applied to both sides.

Place the artwork face down and cover with a piece of tissue larger than the artwork. Wet the tissue completely. The water will penetrate and activate the paste. Cover with nylon netting to prevent the tissue from tearing. Gently remove creases from the center outward using a roller or brush. While drying, it may be necessary to remove the netting and release tension by cutting slits in the excess tissue around the edges. Replace the netting and dry thoroughly between blotters or in a vacuum press.

This naturalization paper was carried by its owner folded in his wallet for 30 years. Although the cellophane tape fell off, the brown stains remain in the paper. The document was supported using a sheer tissue pre-coated with water-based adhesive.

REINFORCING PAINTINGS

FIRST, THE DISCLAIMER

The following techniques are not to be used on any painting that may be considered important or valuable in any way. These methods may not be reversible without irreparable damage to the painting. Also, the identification of the many types of paints, varnishes, fabrics and other materials involved in the making of a painting is difficult. Please call a museum to consult a paintings conservator.

The following methods can be used to support deteriorating paintings on canvas: There are many reasons why the painting is deteriorating; rips, tears, holes, flaking paint, and/or rotting fabric. These conditions can be caused by poor quality materials, poor painting practices, exposure to excessive temperatures, or the fitting of the painting in the frame.

General instruction to reinforce a fabric-backed oil or acrylic painting:

1. Remove the painting from the stretcher bars.

2. Set it face down on a protected surface.

3. Remove dust using a dusting brush, small low-power vacuum cleaner, or compressed air.

4. Cut a piece of fabric larger than the painting. Use a fabric similar to that of the painting. Most paintings are painted on linen or cotton. If unable to identify the fabric, cotton is a safe choice.

DRY MOUNT METHOD

Choose a dry mounting film which will melt into the weave of both fabrics and join them together. Since the adhesive is somewhat soft and elastic it serves well when the mounted fabrics must be stretched over bars.

Put a layer of mounting film between the painting and the new fabric. Line up the fabric grain. Tack the pieces together so they will not shift in the press. Put the layers between two pieces of release paper and place in the press.

Use a sponge sheet as the top layer to prevent the platen from smashing the paint. Once the adhesive has been heated to the correct temperature, remove the mounting package to the cooling table. Immediately weight the package and allow to cool. Place a sponge sheet between the weight and the painting if the painting has dimension. Once the mounted painting reaches room temperature, the painting is ready to be stretched over bars.

WET MOUNT METHOD

Paste selection is important. Several glues or pastes are available in the industry which are specifically made for working with fabric.

Set the backing fabric on a protected surface. Stretch the fabric, using a couple of push pins to hold it somewhat taut. Apply the paste to the backing fabric. Let the paste set up, follow manufacturers directions. Set the painting onto the pasted backing, lining up the grain of the fabrics.

To keep the paint from getting smashed, set a sheet of sponge pad on the top, add a weight and let dry. It may take 12 to 24 hours to dry under a weight. A vacuum press (no heat) will dry the paste in minutes.

ORIENTAL PAPER CUTOUTS

These cutouts are made from very thin white tissue with watercolor on the top surface. The fine areas of delicate paper cannot tolerate aggressive handling; they tear very easily. The open areas do not allow for full sheet adhesives.

The watercolored surface is so sensitive that a damp finger will lift color off the tissue and a too-wet adhesive used on the back may leave a water spot on the front.

Pressure-sensitive hinges and tapes may be used but they will not be removable.

In addition to the handling problems, a customer often requests that the cutout remain flat. Spray mounting will accomplish this. If using glue, tape or hinge methods, explain to the customer the purpose for this choice is to give the cutout a bit of dimension so character of the cutout will be retained, and it will not look like an ordinary reproduction.

It is easy to practice mounting techniques for paper cutouts: simply use a piece of white tissue paper.

SPRAY MOUNTING ORIENTAL CUTOUTS

MATERIALS:
Spray adhesive
Accordion-folded paper support (page 46)
Tweezers
Substrate
Cutout

1. Trim the backing matboard larger than needed. Trimming off the extra later is easier than trying to position the art perfectly.

2. Make an accordion-folded support from paper, large enough to support all parts of the cutout. Lay the cutout face down on the paper support.

3. Shake the spray can well and test the spray to make sure the can is working properly. No globs or particles, only the finest spray will do for this purpose.

4. The cutouts are typically small so one spritz from the can from at least 24" away will produce a light mist of spray glue, which is all that is necessary.

5. Let the adhesive sit for 15 seconds so that it gets tacky.

6. Lift the cutout with tweezers or a palette knife (art supply store) and position the cutout on the substrate.

7. Set a sheet of release paper over the cutout and smooth down. Careful not to be aggressive, or small pieces may break away.

8. Place a weight over the piece and let cure for a couple hours or place in a cold vacuum press.

ALTERNATE METHOD:
Use a pin to apply a small amount of ATG to several spots on the back of the cutout. Lift with tweezers and set on substrate. Tap lightly to secure the adhesive.

Thermographic Prints

Mounting a Thermographic print with Pressure-Sensitive Board

The number of items printed with heat-sensitive inks and/or papers is growing. They may look like ordinary snapshots, even reproductions! They can be difficult to recognize. Many are printed on very thin, slick, opaque paper. The important issue when mounting these items: they cannot withstand heat. They have to be edge-mounted or pressure-sensitive mounted. When in doubt, test a small corner for heat tolerance before heat mounting. Or choose another mounting method, such as the one described here.

MATERIALS:
Pressure-sensitive board
Squeegee or burnisher

1. Clean dust from the item. Be careful when handling—these items tend to be sensitive to fingerprints.

2. To begin, start at one corner, and use a fingernail to carefully lift the release paper to expose a portion of the adhesive. Do not touch the adhesive, as oil from fingers will inhibit adhesion.

3. Place the item on the exposed edge. Carefully pull the release paper from under the item, allowing the work to set on the adhesive surface.

4. Reposition the item until it is in the desired placement. A board which is larger than the artwork may be used and trimmed after mounting.

5. Check for air bubbles by holding the piece up to the light and inspecting the surface. Remove air bubbles by repositioning and smoothing the piece.

6. Set the release paper on the face of the item to avoid scratching the surface. Apply firm, even pressure with a plastic squeegee or burnisher. A mounting press may also be used (no heat necessary).

7. Store the finished piece flat for a minimum of 24 hours to allow the adhesive to cure.

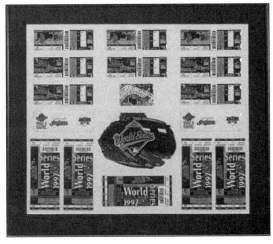

These sports tickets have been edge-mounted, using corner pockets. They were printed with a thermographic printing method and would turn black if heated.

POSSIBLE HEAT-SENSITIVE PRINTING:
- wedding invitations
- award certificates
- event tickets
- electronic imaging papers
- some copier images
- some printer images
- some reproductions

PLAQUES

A mechanical press or a vacuum press can be used to laminate pictures to the surface of wood or fiber board plaques.

MATERIALS:
Mounting Tissue
Laminating Film
Tacking Iron
Acrylic paint
Foam brush
X-Acto® Knife
Art for plaque
Plaquing board

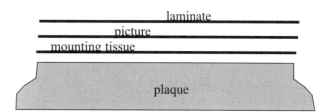

1. Heat the press to the temperature required for the laminate.

2. Trim the print to the size of the plaque surface. Trimming the print face up in a mat cutter creates a reverse bevel that minimizes the white edges of the print paper. For lightweight papers, a straight edge and sharp X-Acto knife can be used instead.

3. Make sure the worktable is clean. Cut a piece of laminate about one inch larger than the print. Place the laminate tacky-side up on the worktable. Brush any surface dust from the print, then place the print face down on the laminate. Smooth the print lightly in place, then flip it face up and smooth out any surface bubbles, lifting the laminate and resmoothing it where necessary.

4. Cut a sheet of mounting tissue about the same size as the laminate. Lay the print face up on the tissue. With a tacking iron placed over a scrap of release paper, lightly tack the mounting tissue to the print and laminate in one corner. Trim the laminate and mounting tissue to the size of the print using a straight edge and X-Acto knife.

5. Paint the edges of the plaque as desired. Two coats may be needed. Varnish if desired. Allow to dry thoroughly.

> ### PAINTING TIP
> Paint the sides of the plaque before mounting. Unless the print paper is thin, don't worry about stray paint on the surface of the plaque—it will not show through the art. For thin papers, paint the plaque surface as well as the sides, so show-through will be an overall, even color.

6. Position the print on the surface of the plaque. Using the tacking iron over a scrap of release paper, tack the print in place at one corner.

7. Cover the assembled materials with a sponge foam overlay and place the unit in a folder of release paper. Place in the press, covered with a foam sheet. Wait for the time recommended by the laminate manufacturer. Remove from press.

TACKING TIP
The plaque may have a hanging area routed out on the back. When tacking the print to the plaque, make sure the hanger is at the top!

TIP
Use perforated laminate with photographs and glossy art to allow trapped air to escape.

MOUNTING TIP
Place the folder of release paper on a piece of mat-board for easier transportation into and out of the press.

Texturizing a Picture

Textures can be added to the surface of a mounted reproduction with a lamination process that uses special texturing film. The finish of the release film (matte or gloss) placed on top of the texturing film determines whether the finish will be shiny or dull.

Texturizing with a Heat Press

The combination of heat and pressure can be used to impress the texture of an artist's canvas or other texture onto the face of the art.

There are many possibilities. A photograph may be given a linen texture. A print may be given the texture of anything from leather to sandpaper. The textures can be transferred from a wide variety of materials.

To Texturize and Mount at the Same Time

Mounting and laminating can be done in one step. The process described here will create a canvas-textured reproduction mounted to canvas.

1. Cut a piece of raw canvas fabric one to two inches larger than the picture to be mounted.

2. On the worktable, make a stack of the materials as follows, starting with the bottom layer:

   > Release paper
   > Artist's canvas fabric
   > Dry mount film
   > Picture, image side up
   > Texturing Film
   > Release Film (Matte or Gloss)
   > Textured material
   > Sponge foam sheet
   > Release paper

3. Follow the texturing film manufacturer's recommendation for the temperature and dwell time.

4. Remove from the press and allow to cool under a weight. When cooled remove the textured material and the matte/gloss release film.

The canvas can now be stretched over stretcher bars like a painting.

To Texturize a Mounted Picture

A picture that is already mounted can be texturized using this process:

1. On the worktable, make a stack of the materials as follows, starting with the bottom layer:

   > Release Paper
   > Mounted Picture, image side up
   > Texturing Film
   > Release Film (Matte or Gloss)
   > Textured Material
   > Sponge Foam sheet
   > Release Paper

2. Follow the texturing film manufacturer's recommendation for the temperature and dwell time.

3. Remove from the press and allow to cool under a weight. When cooled remove the textured material and matte/gloss release film.

Texturizing a Picture Using a Gel

To simulate the texture of an oil painting, brush strokes can be added to the surface of a reproduction using a clear polymer gel typically used by artists to extend their paints. Use Gel Medium (matte or gloss) from Liquitex or Mod Podge® (matte or gloss) by Plaid. The gel may be white upon application but it dries clear.

It is easier to apply brush strokes if the reproduction is mounted to a canvas or mount board because unmounted paper will buckle when the wet gel is applied.

To create realistic brush strokes, use a stiff flat or round bristle brush 1/4" or 1/2" wide. Depending on the brush and the size and pattern of stroke used, many different effects can be created. If working with a reproduction of an oil or acrylic painting, look for the brushstrokes of the artist and try to duplicate the pattern.

Once the brush strokes are complete, allow the gel to dry thoroughly before framing. No glazing is needed—the gel coating serves as a water-resistant protective layer.

APPENDIX A

FAHRENHEIT-CELSIUS CONVERSION TABLE

°F	°C		°F	°C
0	-17.8		125	51.6
5	-15		130	54.4
10	-12.2		135	57.2
15	-19.4		140	60
20	-6.7		145	62.7
25	-3.8		150	65.5
30	-1.1		155	68.3
35	-1.6		160	71.1
40	4.4		165	73.8
45	7.2		170	76.6
50	10		175	79.4
55	12.7		180	82.2
60	15.6		185	85
65	18.3		190	87.7
70	21.2		195	95.5
75	23.9		200	93.3
80	26.7		205	96.1
85	29.4		210	98.8
90	32.2		215	101.6
95	35		220	104.4
100	37.8		225	107.2
105	40.5		230	110
110	43.3		235	112.7
115	46.1		240	115.5
120	48.9		245	118.3
			250	121.1

Using The Chart on the Facing Page

Methods are listed according to the preference of author.

    1 First choice
    2 Second choice
    3 Third choice
    4 Fourth choice
    OK means it is possible but not necessarily appropriate.

- An empty space means the item may buckle, wrinkle, melt, turn yellow, dissolve, or otherwise meet with an unhappy ending.

- Although Spray Adhesive is listed, it is seldom appropriate because the adhesive often contains rubber and/or resin. It has been shown to degrade, turn yellow and loosen over time. The only use the author has for spray adhesive is for the tourist grade paper cutout shown on page 86.

- If an item is valuable it is not appropriate to fully mount it— please use conservation methods, described extensively in *Volume 4, Conservation Framing.*

DISCLAIMER
Deciding whether it is appropriate to mount a particular item is up to the individual framer. This chart suggests mounting methods for many types of artwork and pictures. If a framer has decided a piece should be mounted, this chart provides a list of methods likely to be successful.

APPENDIX B
SUGGESTED MOUNTING METHODS

	Dry Mounting	Wet Mounting	Spray Mounting	Pressure-Sensitive	Laminating	Canvas Transfer	Conservation Methods
	-----FULL MOUNTING METHODS-----						
Bark Painting		2					1
Brass Rubbings	3	2	4	1			1
Certificates (non-animal skin)	1	1	4	1	ok		1
Charcoal Drawings	2						1
Chromogenic Photographs	2	2	4	2	ok	ok	1
Trading Cards (Sports, post, etc.)	1	1	4	2	ok	ok	1
Ilfochrome Classics (Cibachrome)	2		4	3			1
Fabric	1	1	2	1			1
Fiber-Based Photographs	1	1	3	1	ok	0k	1
Fine Art Photographs							1
Heavy Textured Papers	1	1	3	2			1
Giclée/ Iris prints	no						1
Magazine pages	1		4	1	ok	ok	1
Newspaper pages	1		3	1	ok		1
Offset Reproductions	1	1	3	1	ok	ok	1
Oriental Tissue Cut-outs			1				1
Oversized Photographs	1	1	4	1	ok	ok	1
Oversized Posters	1	1	4	1	ok	ok	1
Reproductions	1	1	3	1	ok	ok	1
Parchment/Sheepskin							1
Pen & Ink	1			1			1
Polaroid Prints				1			1
Posters	1	1	3	1	ok	ok	1
Puzzles	1	1	4	1	ok		1
Serigraphs							1
Signed, Limited Editions							1
Silks/Sheer Fabrics	1	2	3	1			1
Snapshots, photographic	1	1	3	1	ok		1
Thermographic printing	no!		3	1			1
Thin Papers/Translucent Paper	1		3	1			1
Pre-Laminated items				1			1
Vellum Animal Skins							1
Watercolor Original							1
Watercolor Paper	1	1		1			1

MOUNTING SUPPLIES
A- ADHESIVES B- BOARDS E- EQUIPMENT

All distributors of framing supplies carry mounting boards, adhesives and equipment. Please ask your distributor for a list of supplies. Many of the companies listed here do not sell directly to the user, rather products are sold through distributors.

Alusuisse Composites Inc. (B)
P. O. Box 507
Benton, KY 42025

American Cardboard Co. (B)
3201 Fox Street
Philadelphia, PA 19129-1835

Crescent Cardboard Co. (A, B)
100 West Willow
Wheeling, IL 60090

Daige Products, Inc. (A, E)
1 Albertson Ave. Suite 3
Albertson, NY 11507

Drytac (A, E)
5373 Glen Alden Drive
Richmond, VA 23231

Drytac Canada Inc. (A, E)
137 Buttermill Ave.
Concord, ON L4K 3X5
Canada

Elmer's Framing Products, Inc./
Bienfang Framing Products
180 E. Broad Street
Columbus, OH 43215

Frame Square Industries
314A Depot Street
Monroe, NC 28112

Gainsborough Products Company
281 Lafayette Circle
Lafayette, CA 94549

Gane Brothers (A)
1400 Greenleaf Ave.
Elk Grove Village, IL 60007

Glue-Fast Equipment Co. (A, E)
727 Commercial Ave.
Carlstadt, NJ 07072-2602

Hartman Plastics Inc. (B)
373 Poplar Road
Honey Brook, PA 19344

Hurlock Brothers Company Inc. (B)
1446-48 W. Hunting Park Ave.
Philadelphia, PA 19140

International Paper (B)
3480 Taylorsville Hwy.
Statesville, NC 28625

Legion Paper Corp. (B)
11 Madison Ave.
New York, NY 10010

Lineco Inc (A)
517 Main Street
Holyoke, MA 01041

Neschen USA LLC. (A)
9800 West York
Wichita, KS 67215

Nielsen & Bainbridge (B)
40 Eisenhower Drive
Paramus, NJ 07652

Parsons Paper (B)
P. O. Box 309
Holyoke, MA 01041

Print Mount Company (A, E)
20 Industrial Drive
Smithfield, RI 02917

Rupaco Paper Corporation (B)
110 Newfield Ave.
Edison, NJ 08837

Savage Universal Corp (A, B)
550 E. Elliot Road
Chandler, AZ 85225
Specialty Tapes (A)
4221 Courtney Road
Franksville, WI 53126-9795

3M Stationery & Office Supplies Div. (A, E)
3M Center
St. Paul, MN 55144-1000

Tru Vue Inc. (A, B)
9400 West 55th Street
Chicago, IL 60525

University Products, Inc. (A)
Main Street
P. O. Box 101
Holyoke, MA 01041

This list does not represent all suppliers. Check listings in trade magazines and association membership listings for more suppliers.

LIBRARY OF PROFESSIONAL PICTURE FRAMING
The Framing Reference Books since 1984!
Updated and Reprinted every two years!
Answers to framing questions at your fingertips!

VIVIAN KISTLER'S
VIDEO WORKSHOPS

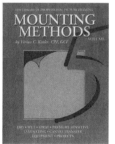

PICTURE FRAMING VOL. 1
by Vivian Kistler, CPF, GCF

Complete overview of custom picture framing – from the equipment to the layout of the shop to the work order processes! History of framing, cutting & joining wood & metal moulding, ordering frames, cutting glazing, measuring, basic mat cuts, mounting equipment & methods, color, proportion of frame design, stretching paintings, conservation. 2002
96 pp   8½x11   B116 $19

MAT CUTTING & DECORATION VOL. 2
by Vivian Kistler, CPF, GCF

Inlays, offsets, double 8-sided mats! Step-by-step directions for 50 + mat cuts; basic to advanced. Measurements, proportion, color selection, fractions, faux finishes, real French mats, hand-cut designs, singles, doubles, v-grooves, color panels, cove mats, fabric wrapped, lattice, multiple opening layouts, Kobe corners, circles, ovals, gothic, fancy corners, 6 & 8 sided, and more! 2001
96 pp   8½x11   B019 $19

FRAMING NEEDLEWORK VOL. 3
by Vivian Kistler, CPF, GCF

Block & stretch needlepoint • 12 methods of mounting textiles • Pins, staples, lacing. A fast method of stretching! Fifteen projects. Types of needlework and fabric. Fabric construction. Pins, needles and such. Cleaning, repairs & pressing. Directions to frame crewel, needlepoint, cross-stitch, antique samplers, quilt, scarf, kimono, carpet, scroll, hanky, doily, Persian art, papyrus, weaving & flag. 2002
96 pp   8½x11   B027 $19

CONSERVATION FRAMING VOL. 4
by Vivian Kistler, CPF, GCF

Handling Art on Paper. Choosing glazing. Making hinges & supports for all types of art on paper. Types of adhesives and matboards. Boards for support. How to deacidify old papers. Encapsulation. Handling problems. Projects. Framing watercolors, papyrus, pastels, photos, skin documents. Techniques for broken and brittle artwork. Cleaning and repairs.   2002
96 pp   8½x11   B035 $19

MOUNTING METHODS VOL. 5
by Vivian Kistler, CPF, GCF

Dry, Wet, Spray and Pressure-Sensitives mounting methods. Types of adhesives, mounting boards. Selecting a process. Bubbles & buckling. Types of equipment. Reversing mounting procedures . Step-by-step projects include: canvas transfer, puzzles, rubbings, cut-outs, fabric, photos, oversized & plastic items. 2002
96 pp   8½x11   B043 $19

FRAMING PHOTOGRAPHY VOL. 6
by Allan Lamb,CPF

Quick Identification Chart. Photography time line. Identify and frame antique photos. Suitable framing methods for: ambrotype, daguerreotype, albumen, tintype, Ilfochrome Classics®, Polaroid®, snapshots and more! Mounting: photos with dry, pressure-sensitive, wet & spray methods. Projects. Creative framing cases. Hinged boxes and montages. 2003
96 pp   8½x11   B051 $19

A FULL SET OF SIX BOOKS FOR ONLY $99!

FRAMING COLLECTIBLES

Building frames, supporting and attaching items. Sports Equipment, Flags, Dried Flowers, Coins, Quilts, Photographs, Stamps, Baptismal Gown, Arrowheads, Toy Train Cars, Bean Bag Animals, Plates, Books, Ceramic Tiles, Marionette, Fans, Diplomas, Marriage Certificate, Puzzles, Seashells, Animation Cels, Perfume Labels, Guns, Tools, Medals.
2000   64pp   8½x11   B299 $19

Color & Design for the picture framer

by Nona Powers, CPF, GCF
Size, color and shape of mats, mouldings and decorative elements. The relationship of color and size, of warm and cool colors and moulding color to mat color. Full-color artworks with different matting selections help you to understand how color and size relate to the framing design.   A workbook with practice sheets is included in the back of the book.
2005   96pp   8½x11   B485 $25

THE ARTICLES OF BUSINESS by V Kistler, CPF, GCF

Advice from the leading expert in the industry! 17 Chapters include: Start up, Credit terms, Finance, Leasing, Volume Framing, PRICING THE CUSTOM PRODUCT, Advertising ideas, , Corporate Sales. 100 *Answers to Expert Questions* include: Location, Merchandising, Personnel, Production, Quality Control, Management, Advertising. Just getting started?--you'll need this book!
192 pp   6 x 9   B280 $20

FLOORPLANS FOR GALLERIES & FRAME SHOPS

by Strasburg-Crawford & Kistler
Maximize your space! 19 floorplans of actual frame shops & galleries. Equipment, lighting, flooring, storage & safety. Front & back room plans for shops from 400 to 4,000 sq.ft. Design your own with grid paper, furniture & equipment patterns included.
32 pp   8½x11   B272 $14

FRAMERS WORK SCHEDULING BOOK

Process orders without losing them! Workflow system with directions for processing frame orders. Schedule work day-by-day. This system neatly records due date, framing info, item location both before & after framing. The spiral bound book lies flat to show the weeks work. Records a full year's work. Provides a record for backup information. Keep the book as historical data.
106 pp   10x13   B124 $19

The Custom Framing Pricing Kit

- 2 PRICE LISTS FOR CUSTOM FRAMING. Convenient, easy-to-use custom framing pricing charts. Printed on heavy paper. 11x14
- 2 VINYL COVERS with a discreet black backing which faces the customer.
- UNITED INCHES WALL CHART 14x17
Updated with higher dollar amounts and footage than earlier versions.
   (English Inch used)
- A large EXPANDED FOOTAGE CHART up to 10 inches wide and 146 United Inches   14x17
- INSTRUCTION BOOKLET
- Moulding Profile Chart   **K949**   **$27**   ©2001

BRIAN WOLF, CPF

DESIGNING & CUTTING MATS

How to design well-proportioned mats. Multi-angles, inlays, v-grooves, decorative carving. Patterns to trace for mat carving, suggested   color combinations for color panel mats. Includes Brian's unique design elements.
B 85X   96 pages   8½x11 $19

HOW TO BUILD FRAMESHOP WORKTABLES, FIXTURES & JIGS

by Paul MacFarland, CPF, GCF
Building plans for 25 projects. Build: Worktables for mat cutters presses, Tool holders, Frame rack, Frame jack, Support for len; moulding, Spool wire box, Roll storage, Bin cart, Tables, To Cabinets, Clamps, Storage for mats, moulding & customer's goods a more! Materials, tools & techniques.
64 pp   8½x11   B361 $19

Just pop it into the computer—select the form you want, customize, if necessary, and **CD-ROMs** *print!* This is not a software application..

CLIP ART FOR PICTURE FRAMERS

Organize, document and simplify the running of your shop with this extensive collection of **printable forms**, labels, and signs designed especially for frame shops and galleries.
©2003   CD663 $15

Ads, Postcards & Counter Cards for Frame shops

Ready-made promotions—military, baby memories, needlework, shadow boxes, kid's art, sports collectibles, Mother's Day, Father's Day, weddings, graduations etc, and a coordinated postcard and counter card for each. Ready to print on your printer—or take them to your local print shop.   ©2003   CD671 $29

Ready-to-Print NEWSLETTERS for Frame shops & Galleries

Thousands of dollars worth of **design, text, photos** and illustrations targeted to your customers. **Ready-to-print** these newsletters will give your shop a professional edge. Each of 4 newsletters covers a variety of topics. 2-page & 4 page newsletters. Color or B&W   ©2003   CD655 $39

BUSINESS FORMS, LABELS & SIGNS for Frameshops & Galleries

Forms include: Application for Employment, Basic Math Skills Test, Consignment Agreement, Cash & Sales Report, Frame Work Orders - 4 versions, Gift Certificate Master Record, , Layaway Master Record, Layaway Tags, Reconciliation of Cash Drawer, Record of Receipt of Artwork, 22 Labels 28 Signs Ready to print. ©2003   CD248 $19

FRAMESHOP REFERENCE POSTERS

Dozens of essential methods--available at a glance. These handy reference posters are made to hang in the framing workshop. Each method is assigned a number and two front counter reference cards containing the list of methods is included with each set of posters, for consistency and coordination between design counter and workshop.Four 11x17 two-color posters with many photos & illustrations. Poster Topics: Needlework & Fabric, Mats & Measurements, Hinges & Supports for Art on Paper and Supporting Collectibles, plus two reference front counter cards.   P078 $20

COLUMBA PUBLISHING COMPANY

2003 W. Market St., Akron, OH 44313
phone 330-836-2619 *or* 800-999-7491
fax 330-836-9659

QTY   NUMBER   NAME   PRICE

_____ _____   _____   _____
_____ _____   _____   _____
_____ _____   _____   _____
_____ _____   _____   _____

All In-Stock Items Shipped the Following Business Day!
Any size order- in US or Canada   SHIPPING $ 4.00
                                        Total _____

MasterCard or Visa, Phone or Fax Charge Orders
Mail Check, Money Order (US funds)
   Order Online: w w w . c o l u m b a p u b l i s h i n g . c o m

Company
_____

Name
_____

Address
_____

City, State, Zip
_____

signature of cardholder   expiration date

phone_____ _____ _____